Capturing the Moment

Capturing the Moment

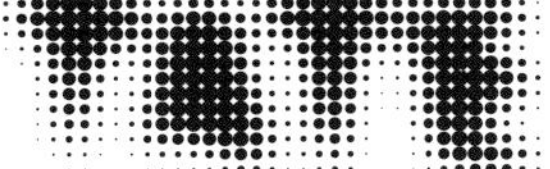

A Journey Through Painting and Photography

'Only photography has been able to divide human life into a series of moments,
each of them has the value of a complete existence.'

– Eadweard Muybridge

'I think that painting is a kind of alchemy. The paint is transformed into image, and paint and image transform themselves into a third and new thing. I want to catch something in the act of becoming something else.'

– Cecily Brown

Director's Foreword

Through a selection of modern and contemporary art, *Capturing the Moment* examines the relationship between the brush and the lens and explores how artists have turned to painting and photography to record moments in time. This exhibition brings together works from the collection of the YAGEO Foundation, as well as Tate's collection of international contemporary art, to show the ways in which the arrival of photography changed the course of painting forever.

Private collections with the richness and depth to make museum-quality exhibitions are few and far between, and we are delighted that our partnership with the YAGEO Foundation has given us the opportunity to present some of the most iconic artworks of recent times, many of which have never before been shown in the UK, and would like to thank the YAGEO Foundation, founded in 1999 by Taiwanese collector, entrepreneur and philanthropist, Pierre Chen, for their kind collaboration. We are thrilled that Tate visitors and a wide readership can now explore the dynamic relationship between painting and photography through these extraordinary works and consider the fascinating connections and questions they inspire.

At Tate Modern, I would like to acknowledge the dedication and expertise of the exhibition curators, Gregor Muir, Director of Collection, International Art, and Beatriz Garcia-Velasco, Assistant Curator, International Art. We are also grateful to Catherine Wood, Director of Programme, Neil Casey, Associate Director, Business and Operations, as well as the whole Tate team across departments. We would like to specially thank colleagues in our Development team for their help in bringing the project to fruition.

We pay tribute to the contributors to this publication for their insights and sensitive readings of individual works and of the exhibition as a whole: Jo Applin, Sean Burns, Brian Dillon, Ismail Einashe, Beatriz Garcia-Velasco, Martin Gayford, Pushpamala N., Amelia Groom, Vanessa Peterson and Barry Schwabsky. We are also indebted to the owners in copyright of the texts reproduced here, most notably Thames & Hudson for permission to include the indispensable interview between Benjamin H. D. Buchloh and Gerhard Richter.

We are grateful to Joe Hales for his inspired design of the publication, which was developed and delivered at lightning pace. Thanks to the Tate Publishing team, most notably Emma Capps, Project Editor, for her careful and attentive contributions and dedicated stewardship, and Bill Jones, Production Manager, for his skilful management of the project through all its stages.

Maria Balshaw, Director, Tate

YAGEO Foundation Foreword

From a young age, attention to detail and the pursuit of quality have been very important to me. This focus and obsession translated to art collecting, which I started at the age of twenty. As a college student, more than four decades ago, I moved from my hometown of Tainan – a small historical town in the south of Taiwan – to Taipei, the country's capital, to study computer science. Within a year, I ended up spending my entire savings on a small wooden sculpture I found at a local art gallery. Over the subsequent decades, my collection has grown, but my original ethos remains. The sculpture is the first work of art I ever bought, and it still sits in my office in Taipei today, reminding me of this marvellous journey.

Following intuition and listening to my own voice have always been at the very core of my approach to collecting. When I started buying art, modern and contemporary works were rare in Taiwan; it was mostly Chinese porcelain and paintings that were making headlines in this part of the world. The only art books readily available to me at the time were auction catalogues, which I read whenever I could. My intuition drew me directly to works of art that were unique and avant-garde. As an engineer working in the electronics industry, I found the creativity and freedom of expression found in modern and contemporary art very refreshing, offsetting my work in a world governed by numbers and logic. In the beginning, I collected both Western and Eastern works of art. Over the years, my business started to grow internationally and took me around the world. It was around this time that I started shifting the focus of my collection to Western art. I looked for works that were original, outstanding and timeless, and developed a collecting strategy based on three main pillars: intuition, analysis and patience. Intuition: how I instinctively feel about the work; analysis: studying the artist's oeuvre and career; patience: investing the time, energy and effort required to acquire them. By following these steps diligently and carefully, I have managed to grow my collection.

In 1999, I founded the YAGEO Foundation as a way to share my passion and collection with the public. The foundation's work focuses on continuing to acquire unique works of art while collaborating with institutions to make sure these works are accessible to a wide and global audience. In the past decade or so, the foundation has had the honour to support and work with many institutions, who each recognise the importance of art in bringing together communities and fostering important dialogues between different cultures and diasporas. It is very exciting to be partnering with Tate to showcase works from their collection in conjunction with the YAGEO Foundation Collection.

Art has a way of transforming our everyday lives – opening doors to new friendships and new ideas. It brings me a lot of joy to be sharing this journey with the world through *Capturing the Moment*.

Pierre Chen, Founder, YAGEO Foundation

The Paradox of the Moment
Beatriz Garcia-Velasco

'Photography's vaunted capture of a moment in time is the seizure and freezing of presence', writes Rosalind Krauss in her seminal text on surrealist photography. 'It is the image of simultaneity, of the way that everything within a given space at a given moment is present to everything else; it is a declaration of the seamless integrity of the real.'[1] *Capturing the Moment* takes its title from a turn of phrase commonly used in relation to photography and, more specifically, to the medium's ability to arrest time and space, creating an image of a present that is necessarily always past. It is a mode of expression that exhausts itself as soon as it is articulated. In the present participle, the phrase underscores the immediacy of the act of 'capturing' while revealing the impossibility, or rather, the inconclusive nature of such a task.

This paradox of the instant is a defining element of photography, one that situates the medium directly in opposition to painting.[2] If the mechanics of the camera work to produce an immediate imprint of reality (what critics have labelled 'indexical': light bounces off an object, passes through a lens and onto a photochemical or digital surface), painting is thought to be, instead, an interpretation of reality, a retrospective enactment of time and space. Addressing this duality, Jeff Wall has commented:

> Part of the poetry of traditional painting is the way it created an illusion that the painting depicted a single moment. In photography, there is always an actual moment – the moment the shutter is released. Photography was based in that sense of instantaneousness. Painting, on the other hand, created a complex and beautiful illusion of instantaneousness. So past, present and future were simultaneous in it, and play with each other or clash. Things which could never co-exist in the world could easily do so in a painting.[3]

Here, photography's claim to the actual stands against the artificiality of painting and its play of impressions and resemblances. Yet Wall, a photographer deeply influenced by the tradition of painting, is interested in challenging the boundaries between perception and representation that bisect both mediums.

Included in this exhibition, *A Sudden Gust of Wind (After Hokusai)* 1993 (see p.62–3) epitomises Wall's approach. To create this work, Wall digitally superimposed more than a hundred photographs taken in an industrially farmed landscape on the outskirts of Vancouver, producing a composition that almost identically mirrors Katsushika Hokusai's (1760–1849) woodcut *Travellers Caught in a Sudden breeze at Ejiri* c.1832. Wall's sprawling photographic tableau depicts four figures seemingly caught in a gust of wind, animated by a swarm of papers and a trilby that have flown away from their owners. This is all, of course, an illusion of simultaneity – to borrow Krauss's term – doubly conveyed by the work's re-enactment of Hokusai's woodcut. By displacing photography from the immediately real and harnessing the drama of fiction, Wall positions the lens in line with the illusions of painting.

It is this 'threshold' that *Capturing the Moment* seeks to open up, bringing together works drawn from the YAGEO Foundation Collection presented in conversation with our holdings at Tate, which together challenge traditional binaries between photography and painting.[4] The exhibition does not (and cannot) offer an encyclopaedic overview of the convergence between these mediums. Instead, it raises a series of prompts, some of which will be addressed in this publication, while others are necessarily left open for the viewer and reader to unpack. Seen together, what underpins this selection of works is a preoccupation with the notion of time (some push at its limits, others hold the moment suspect, calling it into question); an interest in the creative possibilities of truth, untruth and fiction; and a concern with the mechanics of representation and mediation that govern the visual arts.

Creative Actuality

Widely reproduced, Dorothea Lange's 1936 portrait of migrant pea picker Florence Owen Thompson has become an unforgettable image of rural America during the Great Depression – a timeless symbol of human dignity and endurance in the face of hardship (see p.29). The photographers employed by the Farm Security Administration to document the lives of sharecroppers and migratory agricultural workers typically used the camera as a value-neutral lens through which to reveal ontological truths, yet Lange's composition is staged to a painterly effect, and is often compared to religious paintings of the Madonna. Of Cherokee heritage, Owen Thompson remained anonymous until 1978, when she wrote to *U.S. Camera* magazine, where the photograph appeared, stating that she was never consulted by Lange and never gave permission for her image to be used.[5] In as much as the work acquainted metropolitan audiences with the effects of the Depression on rural life, it also reveals, as Susan Sontag put it, Lange's 'own notions about poverty, light, dignity, texture, exploitation and geometry.'[6] Indeed, the idea that photojournalism could offer a transparent image of the world was soon challenged. When Scottish filmmaker John Grierson coined the termed 'documentary' in 1926, he defined it as 'the creative treatment of actuality' – presciently indicating future understandings of how documentary image-making defies categories of fact and fiction, artefact and document, actuality and timelessness.[7]

By the 1930s, photojournalism, broadcast news, illustrated magazines and propaganda posters had a profound influence on the visual arts, including painting (as early as 1867, a documentary viewpoint was evident in Édouard Manet's *The Execution of Emperor Maximilian* series, and later, in Pablo Picasso's monumental *Guernica* of 1937). Similarly, dada, constructivist, futurist, Mexican muralist, and surrealist artists adopted its images and strategies. In Alice Neel's *Puerto Rican Boys on 108th Street* of 1955 (see p.22), we encounter another portrait of the times. In contrast to Lange's photograph, there is nothing pious about the artist's presentation of her subjects: their cool demeanour against a gritty, urban backdrop transmits the rhythms and politics of Neel's New York neighbourhood with a remarkable specificity of time and place. In 1938, Neel had moved to East Harlem, where she documented her neighbours and friends in unsentimental, social realist portraits. 'You know what I thought I'd find there?' she reflected, 'more truth; there was more truth in Spanish Harlem'.[8] Neel described her works as 'pictures' rather than 'portraits', using the brush (to paraphrase the artist) to paint her time and life as it went by.

Today, the prevalence of mass media and news imagery – and, one might add, of manipulated images and fake news – has continued to influence the ways in which painters depict contemporary life. For artists like Paula Rego, Michael Armitage or Miriam Cahn, truth is not found in the space of the real but in the slippage between documentary and fiction. In *War* 2003 (see p.37), Rego draws from a newspaper photograph to portray the aftermath of a bombing in Iraq. Bloodstained creatures contort and scramble in a raging landscape like a sinister fairy tale or a hellish scene in Hieronymus Bosch's *The Garden of Earthly Delights* 1503–15. 'I thought I would do a picture about these children getting hurt, but I turned them into rabbits' heads, like masks', Rego explained. 'It's very difficult to do it with humans, it doesn't get the same kind of feel at all. It seemed more real to transform them into creatures'.[9] Muddled and dark, the pastel is forcefully pushed onto the surface in heavy, violent strokes – a mode of image-making that stands in sharp contrast to the distance and pristine finish offered by photography, and which underscores the nightmarish vision of the moment. In Armitage's depiction of the demonstrations following the 2017 Kenyan general election, the artist's use of *lubugo* (a Ugandan bark cloth traditionally used as a burial shroud) as a support creates a scarred effect across the work's surface through the stitching and irregularities of the material beneath (see pp.96–7). Appropriating the palette of Paul Gauguin's exoticising paintings, Armitage portrays a landscape populated by a jostling crowd of faces, abstract figures and ghostly apparitions, which we also confront in Cahn's *The Beautiful Blue* 2008–17. Each of these paintings takes on documentary subject matter but rejects the cool detachment and transparency of photography in favour of a contingent, embodied materiality.

The Readymade and the Digital

> It seems to me that the invention of the readymade was the invention
> of reality. It was a crucial discovery that what counts is reality, not any
> world-view whatever. Since then, painting has never represented reality,
> it has been reality (creating itself). And sooner or later the value of this
> reality will have to be denied, in order (as usual) to set up pictures of a
> better world.[10]
>
> – Gerhard Richter

To capture the moment is an attempt to hold the moment captive – to acquire,
to confine and to collect time. Indeed, images are not made but taken by the
camera. This acquisitive drive has informed the practice of two important
artists in this exhibition: Francis Bacon and Gerhard Richter, who both zeal-
ously collected found images over decades to use as source materials for their
work. Richter has amassed 5,000 items into an *Atlas* spanning found, personal
and family photographs as well as images from newspapers, books and magazines. The parallels between Aby Warburg's encyclopaedic *Mnemosyne Atlas*
and Richter's are evident, namely in their grouping of images into visual clus-
ters and taxonomies. Warburg's impetus was to map the history of images and
catalogue the ways they reoccur in Western collective memory, a preoccupation into which Richter also seems to be tapping into.

Richter's *Aunt Marianne* 1965 (see p.72), *Barn* 1984, *Venice (Island)* 1985
and *Two Candles* 1982 are all based on photographs – either found, taken by
the artist or sourced from family albums. *Aunt Marianne* adopts the style of
its source material (a black-and-white photograph), portraying a four-month-
old Richter being held by his aunt, who was later murdered by the Nazi eugenics
programme in Dresden during the Second World War. The painting, blurred
with thick horizontal streaks, conveys a disquieting mood; in its opaqueness,
one senses something left unsaid. The persistence of the photographic image
in Richter's paintings articulates the artist's concern with how memory is
captured, collected and transmitted – underscoring the relationship between
image-making, collective memory and historical amnesia.

Richter also dismantles painting's claim to originality and authorial voice
by repositioning the medium into the realm of seriality and multiplicity. As in
Jorge Luis Borges's 1939 short story 'Pierre Menard, Author of the Quixote',
the artist sets out to reproduce what has already been reproduced, mobilising
a play of representations within representations, where the meaning of the
found, ordinary image is re-created, re-interpreted and re-read.

The photographic readymade was, of course, also adopted by pop artists,
who appropriated mass media images and mechanically reproduced them onto
the canvas. Andy Warhol's *Self Portrait* 1966–7 (see p.84) epitomises how pop
captured the new mass subjectivity of the image-world. Here, the self is

packaged as a fetishistic commodity, a simulacral image that is performatively and endlessly spliced, repeated and constructed.

If in the twentieth century the readymade prevailed, by the turn of the century, and with the emergence of computer technology, found images have become a defining element of our information age. Pervasive in our daily lives, images are consumed, edited and shared across the digital realm in new social rituals at an ever-accelerating rhythm. Salman Toor portrays the effects of this incessant bombardment on individual consciousness in *9PM, the News* 2015 (see p.121). In this work, the artist paints a dizzying landscape, where information and digital stimuli seep into the private space of the home and assail a naked male figure, whose fraught psychological state is mirrored by the horizontal plane of the composition, which tilts dangerously under the weight of the media. A specific moment in time – 9pm – seems to unfold endlessly here, warped by the limitless instantaneity of the digital.

Image technologies have radically changed how artists think about and utilise the camera. As the age of mechanical reproduction has given way to the age of digital post-production, artifice – to a greater or lesser extent – is now intrinsic to photography. In the late 1990s, Andreas Gursky and Jeff Wall pioneered the use of digital manipulation in fine-art photography. While Wall uses digital techniques to create a play of illusions, Gursky presents a heightened panorama of contemporary society that cannot be captured by the human eye or the photographic lens.

Paris, Montparnasse 1993 (see pp.56–7) is one of Gursky's first digitally manipulated images, portraying the Mouchotte building as a sprawling, Mondrian-like grid. The work is, in fact, composed of two separate shots of the building – which was otherwise obscured by adjacent construction – that the artist seamlessly merged together. Similarly, the images of individual dancers in Gursky's *May Day IV* 2000 (see pp.58–9) have been spliced and montaged across the composition to portray an endless sea of ravers, a method Gursky also employed to construct the monumental plastic seascape of *El Ejido* 2017 (see pp.54–5). In the detailed artifice of Gursky's images of global capital, mass consumption and popular entertainment, we find the hyperreality and alienation that defines our contemporary condition. Gursky's figures – de-individualised and positioned in vast, painterly fields – confront us with the question of where we stand in this frenzied digital landscape.

Combining painterly materiality with the realm of the digital, Christina Quarles, Laura Owens and Lorna Simpson adopt strategies that challenge the uneasy commingling of gesture and interface. Using Adobe Illustrator to inform and rework the composition of her painting *Casually Cruel* 2018 (see p.125), Quarles creates a pictorial language that is linked to her understanding of identity: queer, entangled and complex. In *Untitled* 2012 (see p.120), one of seven paintings in a cycle displaying the words 'PAVEMENT KARAOKE' across the canvases, Owens similarly combines intuitive and mediated gestures, layering silkscreen prints of newspapers, painted grids and sections of gingham cloth beneath thick strokes of extreme impasto that follow a shape generated by the artist using Photoshop. The large letters spanning six of the seven canvases, with 'RA' visible in this edition, are 'cutouts' of the lines of small print taken from the classifieds in the 1960's countercultural newspaper *The Berkeley Barb*. The words fade in and out of view, obscured and camouflaged inside the dense undergrowth of marks that Owens has woven across the image plane. Owens integrates the analogue and the digital to propose a new mode of mark-making that, for the artist, is explicitly feminist, rejecting the masculine gestures and 'heroic' immediacy associated with abstract expressionism. What her marks generate, instead, is a vertiginous picture plane made electronic puzzle in which materials, textures and information appear to recede into and expand out of the canvas, momentarily distorting our perception of space and time. 'I feel that the artwork is co-created by the viewer', Owens explains, 'I have always thought of it that way'.[11]

In *Then & Now* 2016 (see p.122), Simpson weaves together the materiality of the canvas, the screen and the body to address police brutality and structural violence against Black Americans. To make this work, the artist digitally enlarged two archival photographs of the 1967 Detroit uprising and screenprinted them onto a support made up of twelve clayboard panels, then added drips of black ink by hand. It is telling that Simpson reconfigures press images of a key moment in the history of the civil-rights movement by both mechanical and gestural means. The former alerts us to the apparatuses and practices that historically mediate and police Black bodies, which are here surveilled from above and pictured in direct opposition to the armed police (or the normative order). The latter are the artist's marks of expression and selfhood, forcefully conveying the experience of being in the moment – in the world. Today, as viral images and footage of police brutality circulate worldwide with the increased influence of the Black Lives Matter movement, the work takes on a new resonance, asking how bodies relate to the mediated fabric of screen, image and user. This idea takes full force with the development of artificial intelligence and its impact on painting and photography, which necessarily calls for a reassessment of the structures that underpin the act of image-making.

Simpson shatters the distance between then and now to underscore the continuing violence inflicted upon Black lives half a century after the work's source photographs were taken. The work resonates with what Christina Sharpe calls the 'orthography of the wake': 'To be in the wake is to occupy and to be occupied by the continuous and changing present of slavery's as yet unresolved unfolding', Sharpe theorises.[12] 'In the wake, the past that is not past reappears, always, to rupture the present'.[13]

'The painter constructs, the photographer discloses.'

– Susan Sontag

Painting in the Time of Photography

Throughout the twentieth century, the idea that painting accurately mirrors the world was complicated by artists' use of photography. Lens-based media could offer a much more convincing representation of reality than painted canvas. Painters developed new styles and perspectives in response to this challenge, particularly when exploring the human figure.

Lucian Freud and Francis Bacon use the human form to expose the visceral reality of the self. Whereas Freud preferred to paint from life, Bacon draws from photographic material. He violently distorts the human figure to reveal what he called 'the pulsations of a person'.[1] Pablo Picasso had also challenged notions of painterly representation and linear perspective to develop a style known as cubism. In these portraits he collapses multiple perspectives into one single moment in time.

Alice Neel and Dorothea Lange aim to depict the social realities of their time through emotionally charged portraits. Neel records everyday life in a working-class New York neighbourhood, painting people as they really are. Lange takes up similar themes through photography, documenting the US Great Depression in emotive portraits of farm labourers in Southern California.

'My object in painting pictures is to try and move the senses by giving an intensification of reality.'

– Lucian Freud

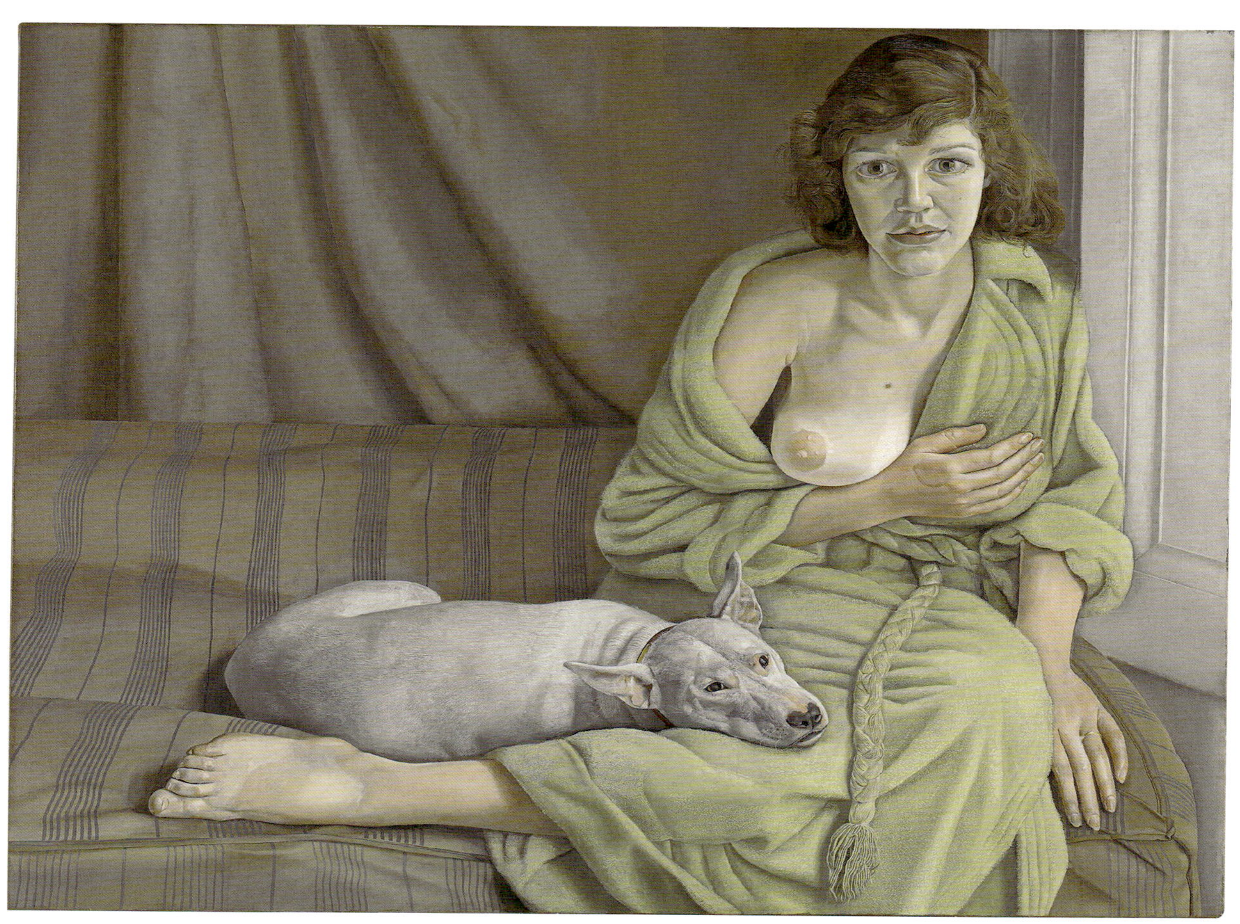

Lucian Freud
Girl with a White Dog 1951–2 Oil paint on canvas, 76·2 × 101·6 mm
Tate, purchased 1975

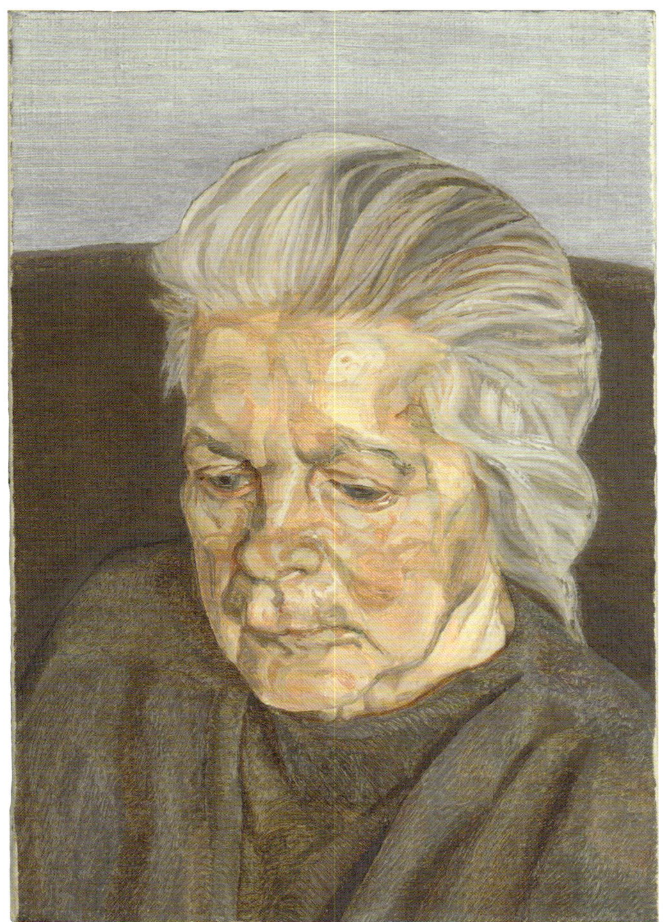

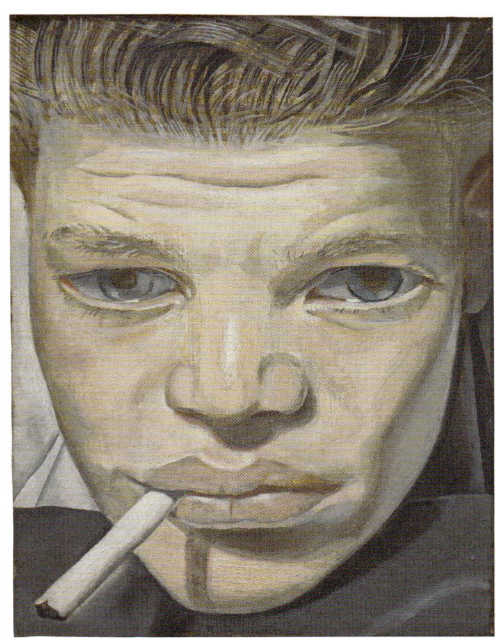

The Painter's Mother IV 1973 Oil paint on canvas, 273 × 186 × 16 mm
Boy Smoking 1950–1 Oil paint on copper, 155 × 115 × 2 mm
Tate, bequeathed by Simon Sainsbury 2006, accessioned 2008

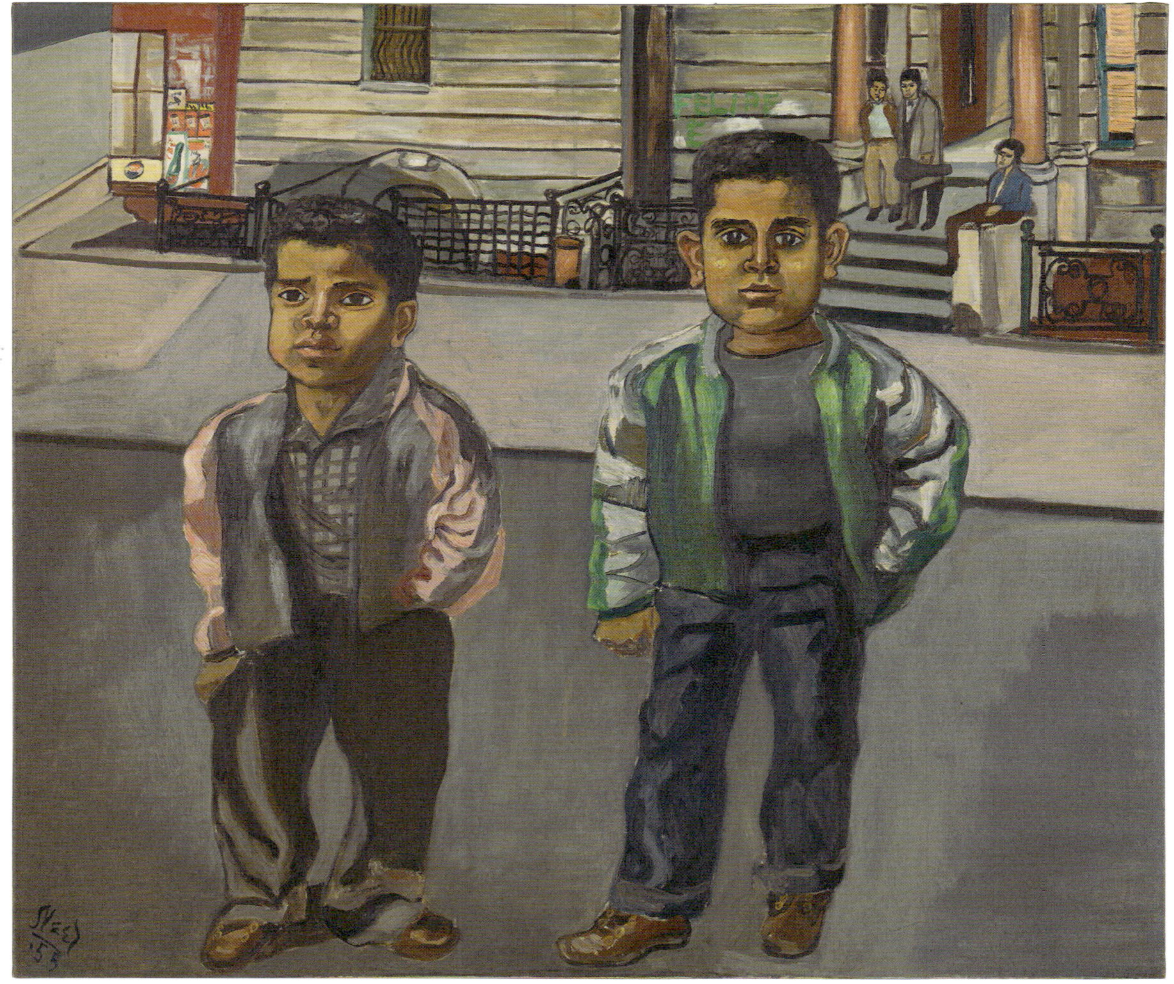

'I paint my time using the people as evidence.'

– Alice Neel

Alice Neel
Puerto Rican Boys on 108th Street 1955 Oil paint on canvas, 1066 × 1221 mm
Tate, presented by the American Fund for the Tate Gallery, courtesy of Hartley and Richard Neel, the artist's sons 2004

Alice Neel
Puerto Rican Boys on 108th Street 1955
Amelia Groom

> I love you Harlem / Your life your pregnant / Women, your relief lines / Outside the bank, full / Of women who no dress / In Saks 5th Ave would / Fit, teeth missing, weary, / Out of shape, little black / Arms around their necks / Clinging to their skirts / All the wear and worry / Of struggle on their faces / What a treasure of goodness / And life shambles / Thru the streets, / Abandoned, despised, / Charged the most, given / The worst / I love you for electing / Marcantonio, and him / For being what he is / And for the rich deep vein / Of human feeling buried / Under your fire engines / Your poverty and your loves [1]

Untitled, undated and unpublished in her lifetime, the above poem by Alice Neel is a clear testament to the love she felt for the uptown Manhattan neighbourhood where she lived for several decades. It was 1938 when Neel moved from Greenwich Village to East Harlem – also known as Spanish Harlem or El Barrio – with her then-lover José Santiago Negron, a Puerto Rican musician. The romantic relationship didn't last, but Neel's love for the working-class immigrant neighbourhood did. *Puerto Rican Boys on 108th Street* is one of the many street scenes she painted during the 1940s and 1950s, showing neighbours, friends, tenement exteriors, corner stores and the life that, as she wrote, 'shambles / Thru the streets'.

When she painted these anonymised 'Puerto Rican Boys', Neel had been living on welfare and raising her two sons on her own.[2] She painted constantly throughout her life, but widespread appreciation for her work would only come much later, thanks in large part to the feminist art movement. Neel had her first retrospective at the Whitney Museum of American Art, New York in 1974, when she was seventy-four years old. In earlier decades she sold very few paintings, and many had never been exhibited. Her apartment was also her studio and the place where she stored all her work, and the art critic Robert Storr has described the sense of 'sedimented painting' that could be felt in this space, with many layers of history – all these pictures, 'all these people' – stacked up against the walls.[3]

Neel was deeply committed to emancipatory politics. She painted portraits of union leaders and civil rights activists, and published illustrations in the American Marxist journal *Masses & Mainstream*. In 1951, the Communist writer Mike Gold organised an exhibition of Neel's work, describing her in the catalogue essay as a 'pioneer of socialist realism in American painting'.[4] Her

'I love you Harlem' poem mentions her love for Vito Marcantonio, the socialist congressperson who represented East Harlem and was an avid supporter of working-class, immigrant and African American civil rights.

In 1955, the same year she painted *Puerto Rican Boys*, Neel was interviewed twice by the FBI, whose files show that she was under investigation for several years due to her periodic involvement with the Communist party (though she was never an official member). A former acquaintance had contacted the FBI to inform them that Neel was an 'avowed, uninhibited' Communist. The outraged informant declared that Neel had a reputation for being 'a swine in human form', and that she was stubbornly '"fixed" upon equal rights for all the coloured, yellow, and brown races via Communistic ways and ideas for these races'.[5]

Critics have often noted that one of the ways Neel went against the grain of her time was that she painted figuratively right throughout the reign of abstract expressionism – a time when, in Neel's words, 'they wouldn't let people-painters even get a foot in the door'.[6] Clement Greenberg, the modernist critic who was at the helm of the abstract expressionist movement, had insisted that painting needed to differentiate itself from photography by transcending depiction and becoming 'pure'. This was during the Cold War; historians have since revealed the extent to which abstract expressionism was instrumentalised and indirectly funded by the CIA in an attempt to pit the ideology of American 'freedom' against the Soviet Union's mandate that artists conform to socialist realism.

While Neel was a (small c) communist and, as she put it, a 'people-painter', she also went against the dominant grain of socialist realism, in that she eschewed heroic depictions of the able-bodied male worker and instead painted women, children, sick people, pregnant people, overtly queer people and other outcasts who had rarely made it into the frame of conventional portraiture.

How should we look at *Puerto Rican Boys* in the context of *Capturing the Moment*, an exhibition that explores the relationship between painting and photography? Comparisons between these media often posit photography as the more objective of the two, insofar as it can capture whatever appears before the lens. This familiar characterisation can be complicated through investigation of the ways that photographic pictures are in fact loaded with subjectivity; questions about what the photographer allows into the frame and how they relate to what they are photographing can remind us that the photographic encounter is never neutral. In the case of Alice Neel, though, we have the inverse to this line of inquiry, because she would claim, surprisingly, that her paintings were 'quite objective'.

'One of the reasons I painted', Neel once remarked, 'was to catch life as it goes by, right hot off the griddle'.[7] When the art historian Cindy Nemser asked Neel if she put a lot of herself into her paintings, she replied, 'I think they're quite objective, don't you?'[8] The writer Hilton Als has said that Neel's paintings often make him think of jazz musicians like Cecil Taylor, who insisted on an openness to the world. Als recounts how, once, someone was trying to stop a child in the recording studio from playing with a ball, and Taylor said, 'no, don't do that, that's what's happening now, that's part of the recording, that's part of the experience'.[9]

This principle of remaining open to whatever was happening *in the moment* is palpable in *Puerto Rican Boys*, which has a quality of spontaneity reminiscent of a photographic snapshot. Consider the group of people hanging out on the stoop in the background; these three East Harlem neighbours seem to be looking over at the encounter between Neel and the boys, giving the impression that we are witnessing a fleeting moment, and that the scene has been permeated by the contingencies of the street.

At the same time, Neel's paintings are also incredibly painterly. She invites us to think of them as 'quite objective', and in doing so, she proposes a new kind of objectivity – a wonky objectivity that is full of idiosyncrasy and awkwardness. Her subjects might appear amid strange patches of negative space. Proportion is often wayward. She makes her figures radiate with intensity by painting areas of high-contrast colour around their edges, as we see in this work, where the grey of the pavement becomes lighter around the boys' bodies. Many of her later subjects vibrate with electric blue outlines. 'I paint my time using people as evidence', Neel said.[10] But she had a thoroughly particular way of looking at – and being in – her time. 'Should thoughts be said plain', she once mused in her notebook, 'or wasn't it more fun to play hide and seek – to hide them artfully in little corners?'[11]

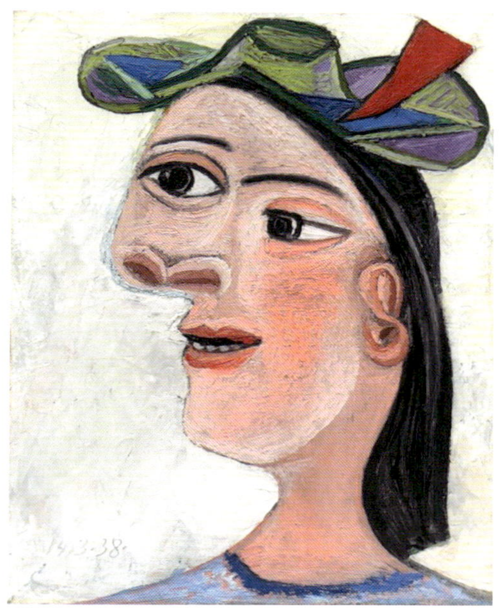

'Photography has arrived at the point where it is capable of liberating painting from all literature, from the anecdote, and even from the subject. In any case, a certain aspect of the subject now belongs to the domain of photography. So shouldn't painters profit from their newly acquired liberty, and make use of it to do other things?'

– Pablo Picasso

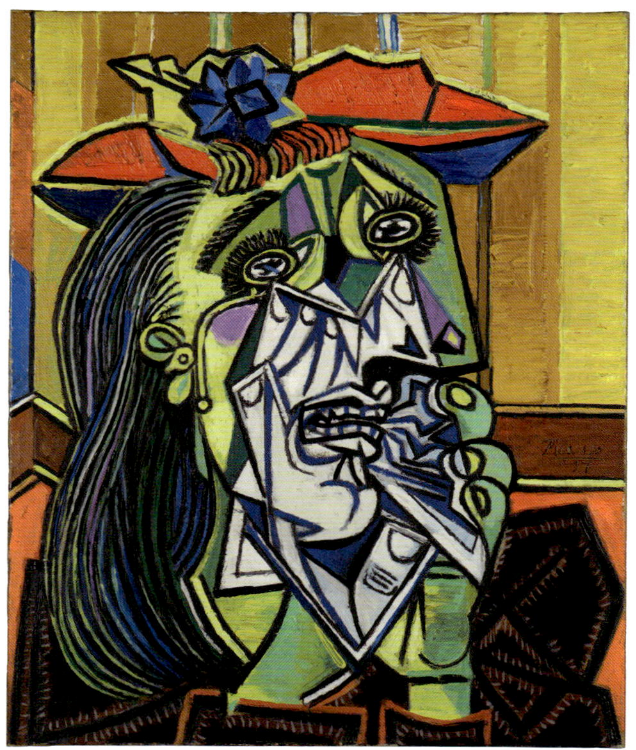

Pablo Picasso

Bust of a Woman (Buste de femme) 1938 Oil paint on canvas, 460 × 380 mm
YAGEO Foundation Collection, Taiwan

Weeping Woman (Femme en pleurs) 1937 Oil paint on canvas, 608 × 500 mm
Tate, accepted by HM Government in lieu of tax with additional payment (Grant-in-Aid) made with assistance from the National Heritage Memorial Fund, the Art Fund and the Friends of the Tate Gallery 1987

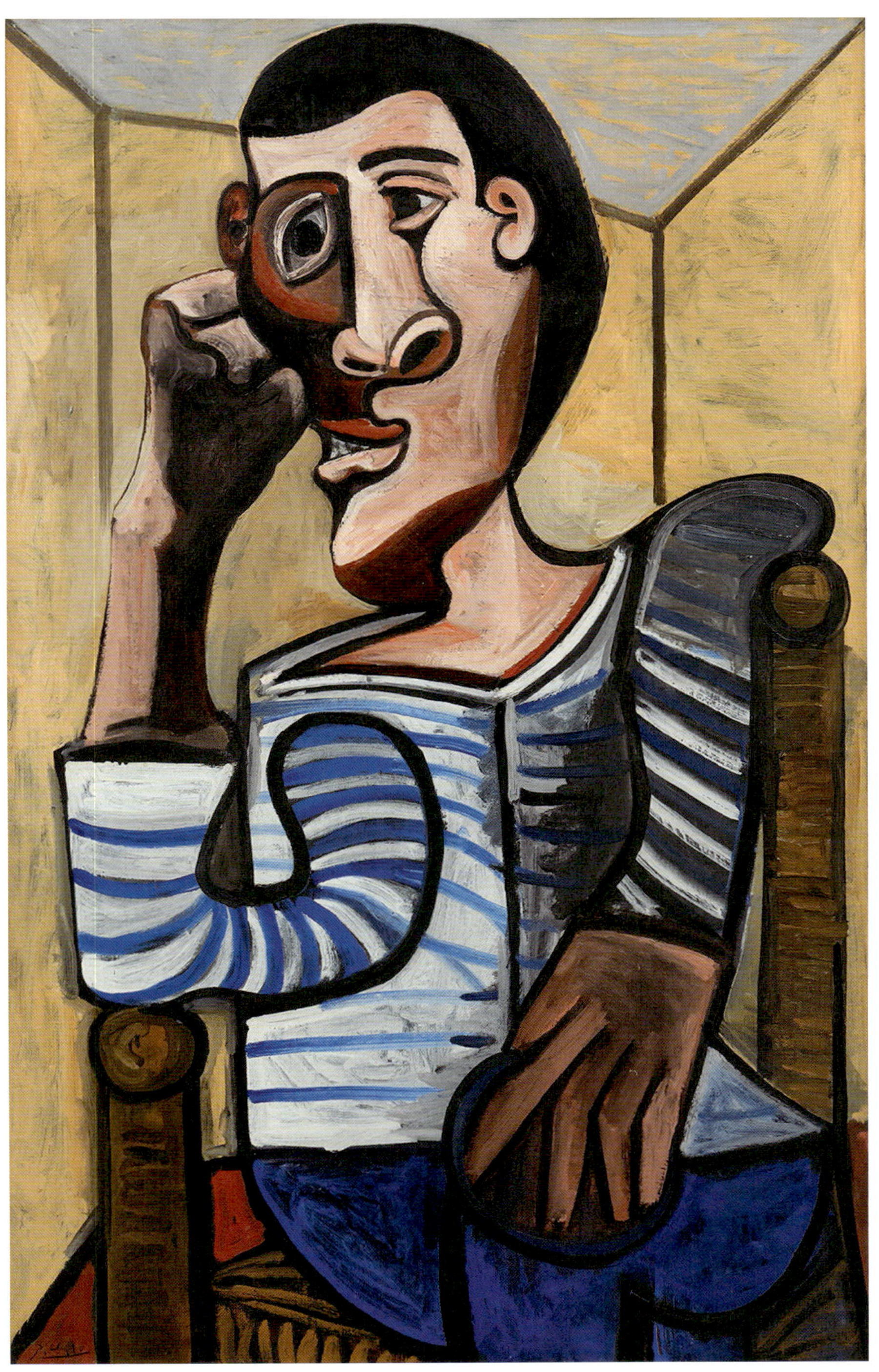

The Sailor (Le Marin) 1943 Oil paint on canvas, 1318 × 806 mm
YAGEO Foundation Collection, Taiwan

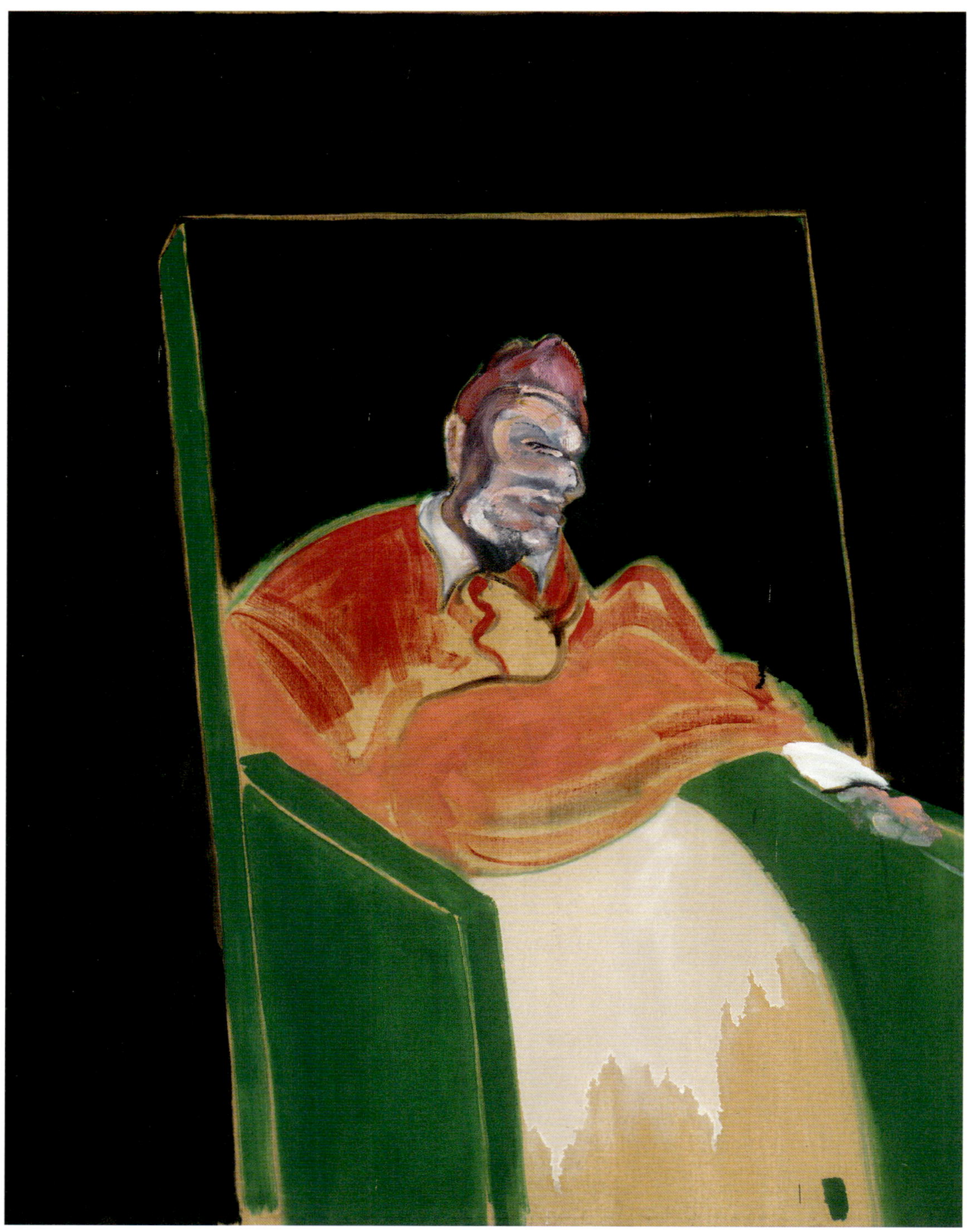

Francis Bacon
Study for Pope VI 1961 Oil paint on canvas, 1525 × 1168 mm
YAGEO Foundation Collection, Taiwan

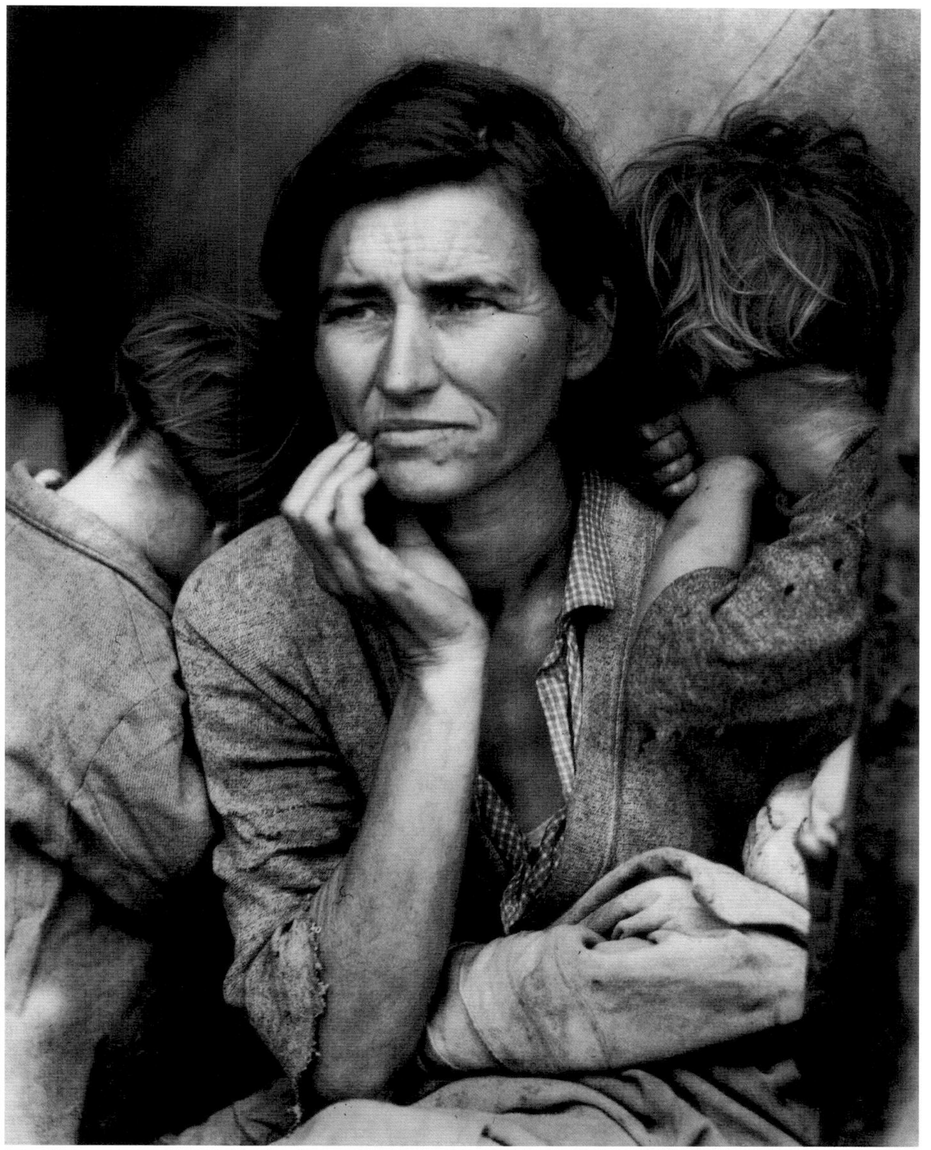

'Bad as it is, the world is potentially full of good photographs.
But to be good, photographs have to be full of the world.'
— Dorothea Lange and Daniel Dixon

Dorothea Lange
Migrant Mother, Nipomo, California 1936 Photograph, gelatin silver print on paper, 355 × 280 mm
Tate, accepted by HM Government in lieu of inheritance tax from the Estate of Barbara Lloyd and allocated to Tate 2009

Tensions

While photographers grapple with the mechanics of the camera, painters continue to work with the surface of the canvas and the texture of paint. They often want to explore the material possibilities of the medium, as well as the painted image itself. The artists in this chapter harness the expressive power of painterly materials and techniques. They create layered compositions that privilege abstract sensations over depictions of reality.

In Francis Bacon's work every brushstroke is emotionally charged. He approaches the act of painting as an assault upon the human form, creating images of a complex and tormented inner self. Similarly, Paula Rego's painterly technique forcefully expresses the violence of her subject matter.

Breaking down the human figure, Cecily Brown asks questions about how paint can convey the essence of bodies or figures. Can the texture of paint itself transmit the rawness and vibrancy of human flesh? Can painted images, as Bacon, Marwan and George Condo suggest, embody the multiple, fractured facets of the mind? Turning the canvas upside down and upsetting the visual order, Georg Baselitz asks that we look closer, not at the figures but at the painted surface instead. Material, expressive painting such as this resists the precision of the mechanical eye and a world increasingly filled with photographic imagery.

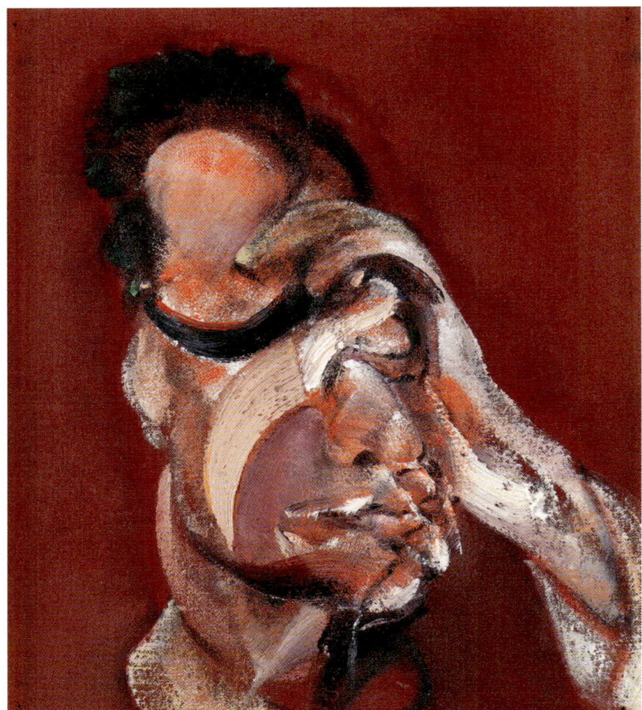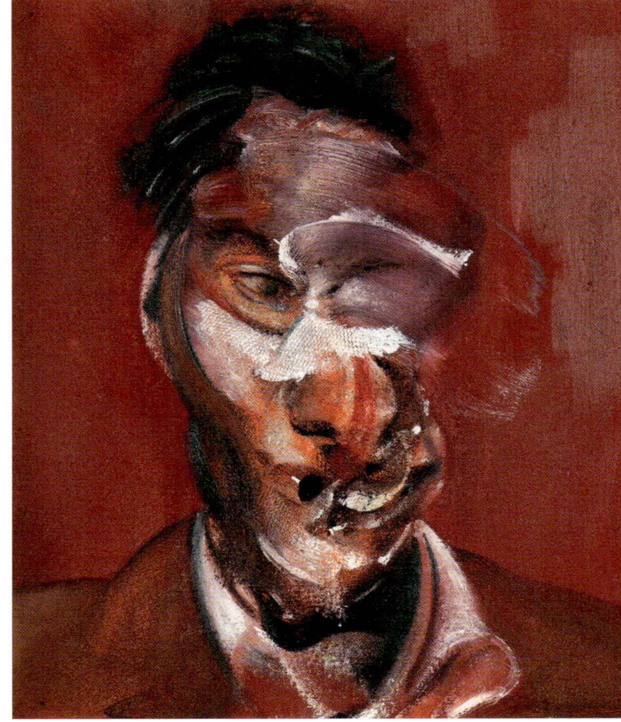

Francis Bacon
Three Studies for Portrait of Lucian Freud 1965 Oil paint on canvas, each 335 × 305 mm
YAGEO Foundation Collection, Taiwan

Francis Bacon
Three Studies for Portrait of Lucian Freud 1965
Sean Burns

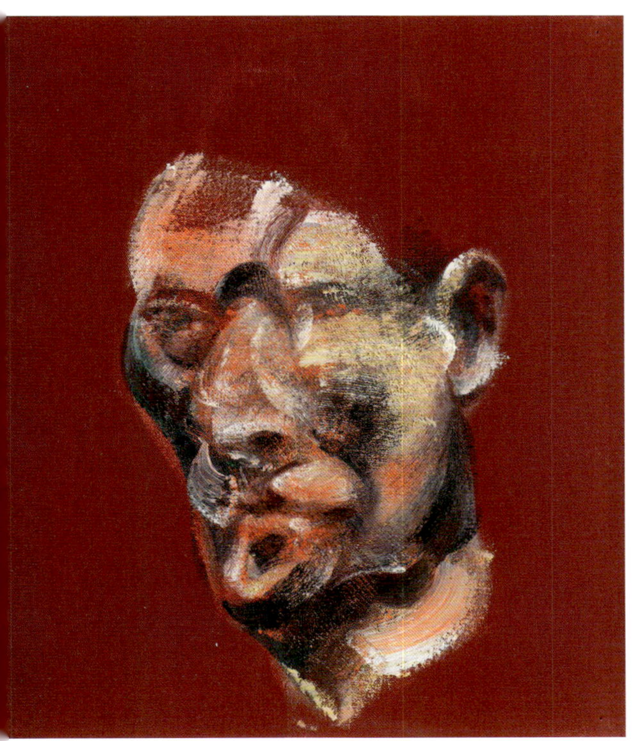

Francis Bacon and Lucian Freud first met through the artist Graham Sutherland in 1944, as the war was ending, and the two quickly became regular drinking and gambling buddies. As Britain's most notable post-war figurative painters, they each shared a fixation on the body, and their pictures – although vastly different, with Freud's fastidious penchant for detail and Bacon's impulsive brushwork – often contained a stark sense of alienation.

Bacon and Freud inhabited a London marred by war and financial hardship. Their haunts were often raucous watering holes teeming with boisterous imbibers, such as the infamous Colony Room Club and Gargoyle Club. Among other regulars was John Deakin, a *Vogue* staff photographer who was notoriously hired and fired twice for his cantankerous behaviour.[1] In early 1963, Deakin staged a lunch (for an unused commission) at Wheeler's, an oyster bar on Old Compton Street, and photographed Bacon and Freud alongside Michael Andrews, Frank Auerbach and Timothy Behrens – a group of artists that R. B. Kitaj would later refer to as the School of London.[2] The negatives from that day offer a rare glimpse into the interplay between these great painters. Bacon was thirteen years older than Freud, and no doubt fostered the younger artist's talents and addictions. Lady Caroline Blackwood, who was married to Freud from 1953 to 1959, remembered having dinner and lunches with Bacon 'nearly every day'.[3]

By 1953, Bacon had established his signature style of agitated markings, swirling figures and ghostly architectural shapes rendered in emphatic reds, oranges and greens. His unflinching pictures drew from his life, as well as the books and scraps of paper that cluttered his studio. He voraciously collected reference images from varying sources, including surgical and zoological books, art-history catalogues and newspapers. Take, for example, Bacon's celebrated *Study after Velázquez's Portrait of Pope Innocent X* 1953, in which he unites two source images: Velázquez's original painting from c. 1650 and a still from Sergei Eisenstein's Soviet silent film *Battleship Potemkin* from 1925, in which an older woman silently screams as a bullet shatters her *pince-nez*. By collaging two disparate but evocative signifiers, Bacon seems to suggest that Velázquez's pope contains within him the horror and isolation that Eisenstein's bespectacled woman exudes. Rather than capturing or translating a single moment in the way a photograph might, Bacon's paintings were more about eliciting the energy and aura of a subject or scene. While photographs often condense reality, Bacon seemingly sought to explode it.

In the 1950s, Bacon began to divest from biblical iconography and focus on his social set, distilling his subjects' spirits and conveying a harrowing sense of disintegration through sweeping, painterly gestures. Perhaps out of compassion for Deakin, a chronic alcoholic who struggled to hold down paid work, Bacon commissioned him to take photographic portraits to use as source materials for paintings.[4] For around a decade from 1960, Deakin produced several series of portraits of the artist's inner circle, including Bacon's lovers Peter Lacy and George Dyer; his close friend, the artist and set designer Isabel Rawsthorne; the muse, memoirist and Soho fixture, Henrietta Moraes; and Freud.[5]

Between 1951 and 1971, Bacon painted sixteen portraits of Freud, which reveal the closeness the two artists shared. (Freud, who worked from life, would paint Bacon twice.) In 1964 and 1965, Bacon produced two triptychs, both rendered in his signature blood-red crimson and titled *Three Studies for Portrait of Lucian Freud*. In both works, Freud's eyes seem opaque – closed or directed out of frame. The earlier version depicts Freud compressed in a cubist blending of perspectives, his face caught in dashes of white, pink, black and green; in two of the panels, an ominous doorway looms behind him. In the 1965 study, the crimson has entirely engulfed the background.

Before it, Freud emerges in thick streaks of orange, white and pink, somehow more precarious and impressionistic than the earlier study. In both, Freud brings his hand to his forehead as if fending off Bacon's gaze.

Although the two artists were practically 'inseparable' during the 1950s and '60s, by the early 1980s, their relationship had become strained.[6] By 1985, it was entirely over.[7] Though it is often said that Bacon criticised Freud's social climbing and meticulousness,[8] recordings of a conversation between Bacon and his close friend and neighbour, the writer Barry Joule, suggest Freud 'cut Francis off' because he was jealous.[9] The breakdown of their relationship was also presumably compounded by Freud's refusal to loan Bacon's 1953 masterpiece *Two Figures* (which he had bought from Bacon through the critic David Sylvester for just £60) to any exhibitions, which utterly enraged Bacon.[10] In 1985, Nicholas Serota, then the director of the Tate, requested the work from Freud to be used in a major retrospective, but Freud declined, much to Bacon's upset.[11] Shortly before he died in 1992, Bacon described the end of his relationship with Freud as 'rather sad'.[12]

When Bacon passed away in 1992, his entire estate, including his studio at 7 Reece Mews, was left to his young companion, John Edwards, whom Bacon had met several years earlier while Edwards was working as a barman. In the early 2000s, Edwards entrusted the property to the Hugh Lane Gallery in

Dublin, where Bacon was born. This decision led to an unprecedented modern-day archaeological exercise in which the studio and its entire contents (including the dust) were carefully uprooted and transported to the gallery to be frozen in time. The studio's extensive textual materials – including photographs, paint-splattered newspaper pages and creased reproductions of works by artists including Pablo Picasso and Velázquez – offer valuable insight into the veiled construction of Bacon's eclectic images. In an episode of the British television series *The South Bank Show* in 1985, Bacon told the presenter Melvyn Bragg, 'You can't make illustrations anymore because they're done much better by cameras and cinema ... I create images that concentrate on reality and are a shorthand of sensation'.[13] Never wanting to mimic the way his subjects were captured by the camera, Bacon employed paint to complicate, collage and transform the photographs from which he worked into something altogether more real.

'When you draw you can push your pencil
or your pastel – everything is much more
violent. Painting is much more lyrical.
That's why I took up pastel and haven't
given it up.'

– Paula Rego

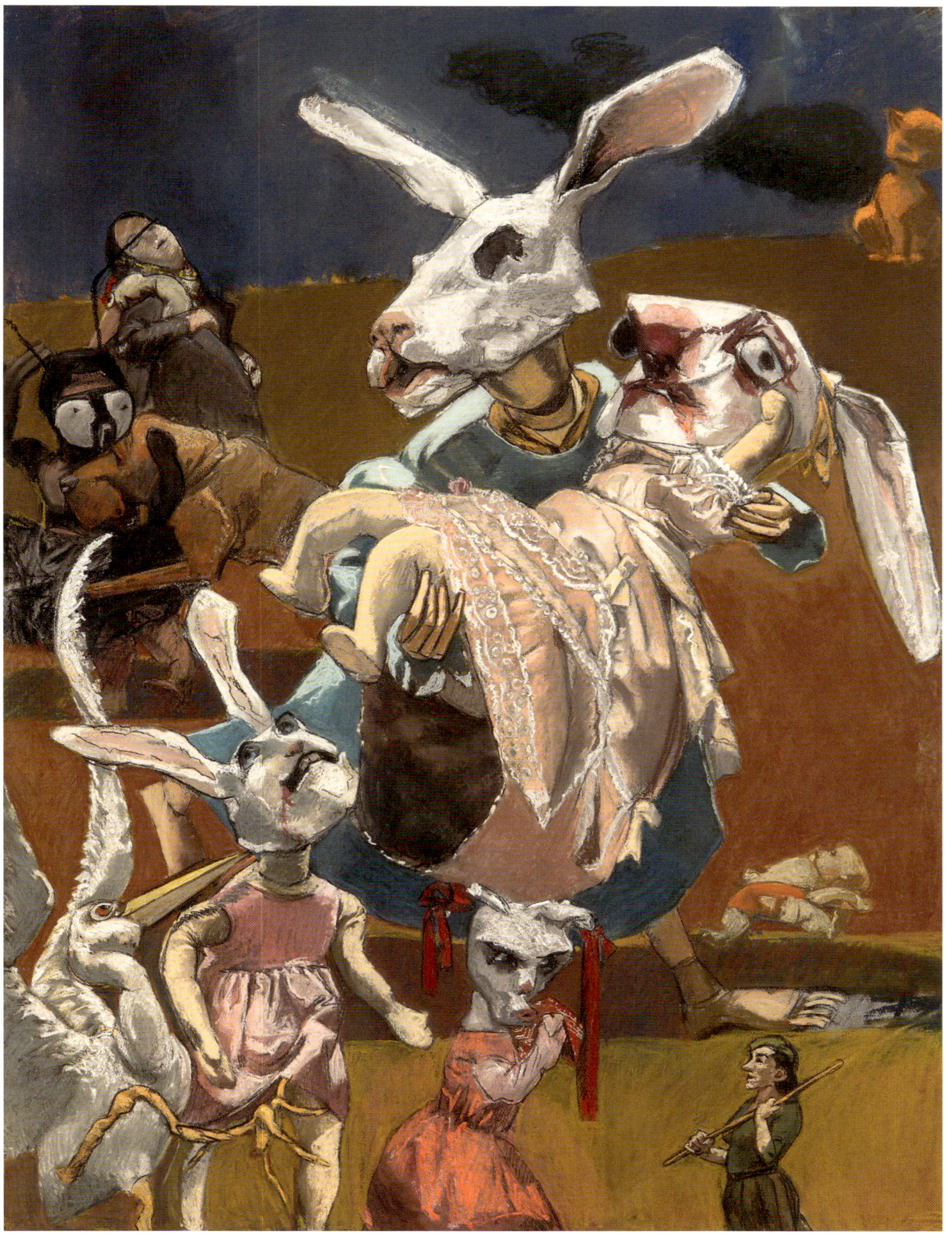

Paula Rego
War 2003 Pastel on paper on aluminium, 1743 × 1343 × 60 mm
Tate, presented by the artist (Building the Tate Collection) 2005

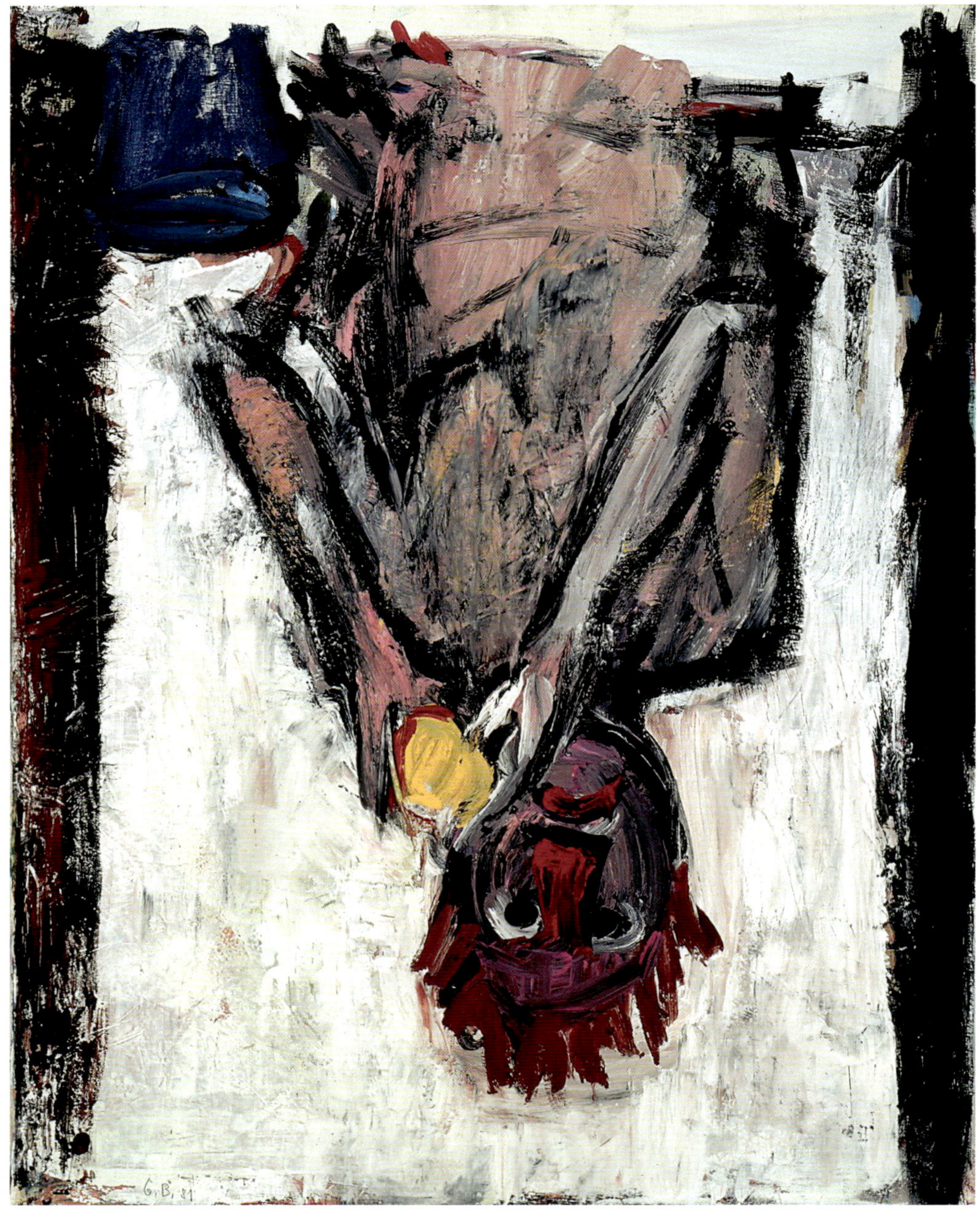

Georg Baselitz
Orangenesser II 1981 Oil paint on canvas, 1460 × 1140 mm
YAGEO Foundation Collection, Taiwan

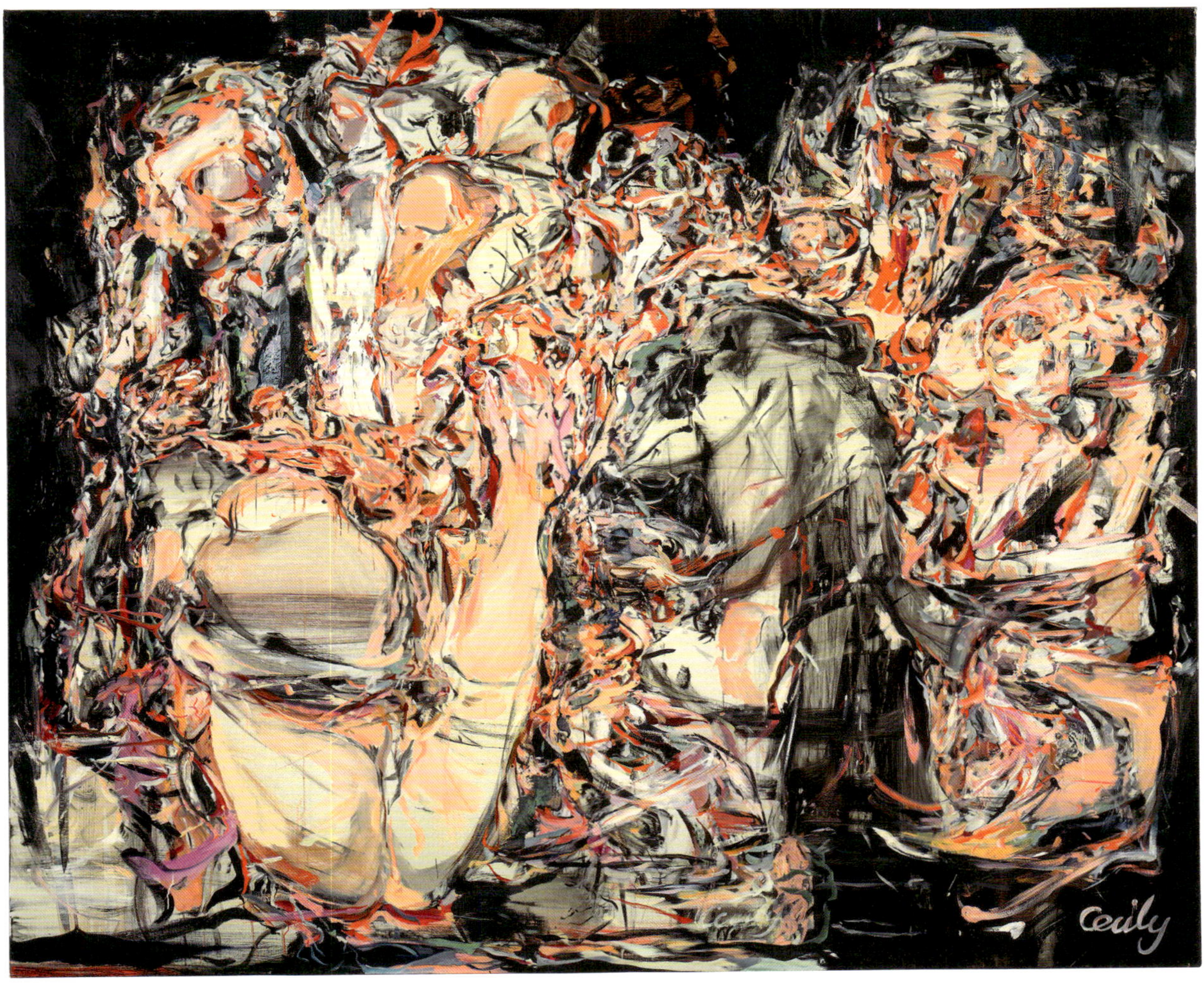

Cecily Brown
Trouble in Paradise 1999 Oil paint on canvas, 1912 × 2293 × 51 mm
Tate, purchased 2000

'I describe what I do as psychological cubism. Picasso painted a violin from four different perspectives at one moment. I do the same with psychological states.'

– George Condo

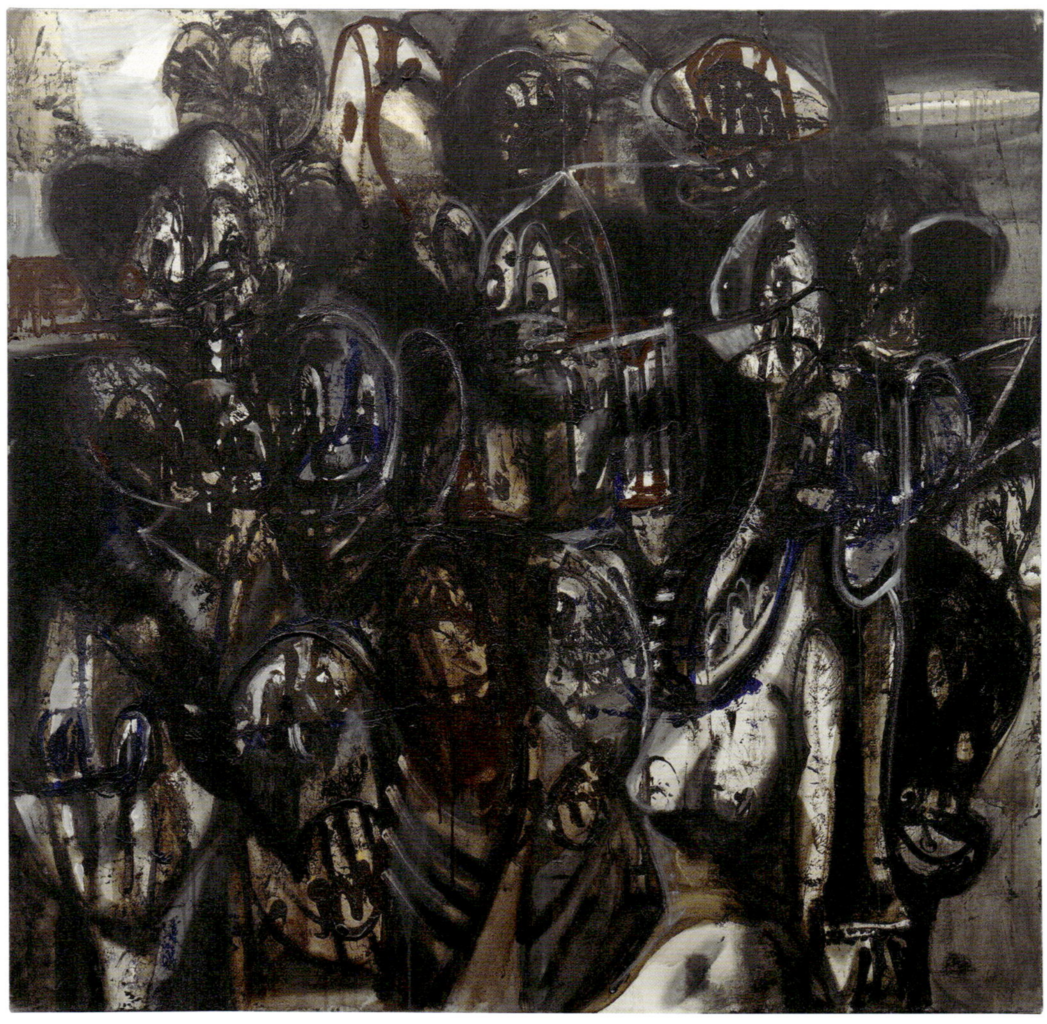

George Condo
Mental States 2000 Oil paint on canvas, 1322 × 1324 × 33 mm

 Tate, purchased with assistance from the Karpidas Family (Tate Americas Foundation) 2015

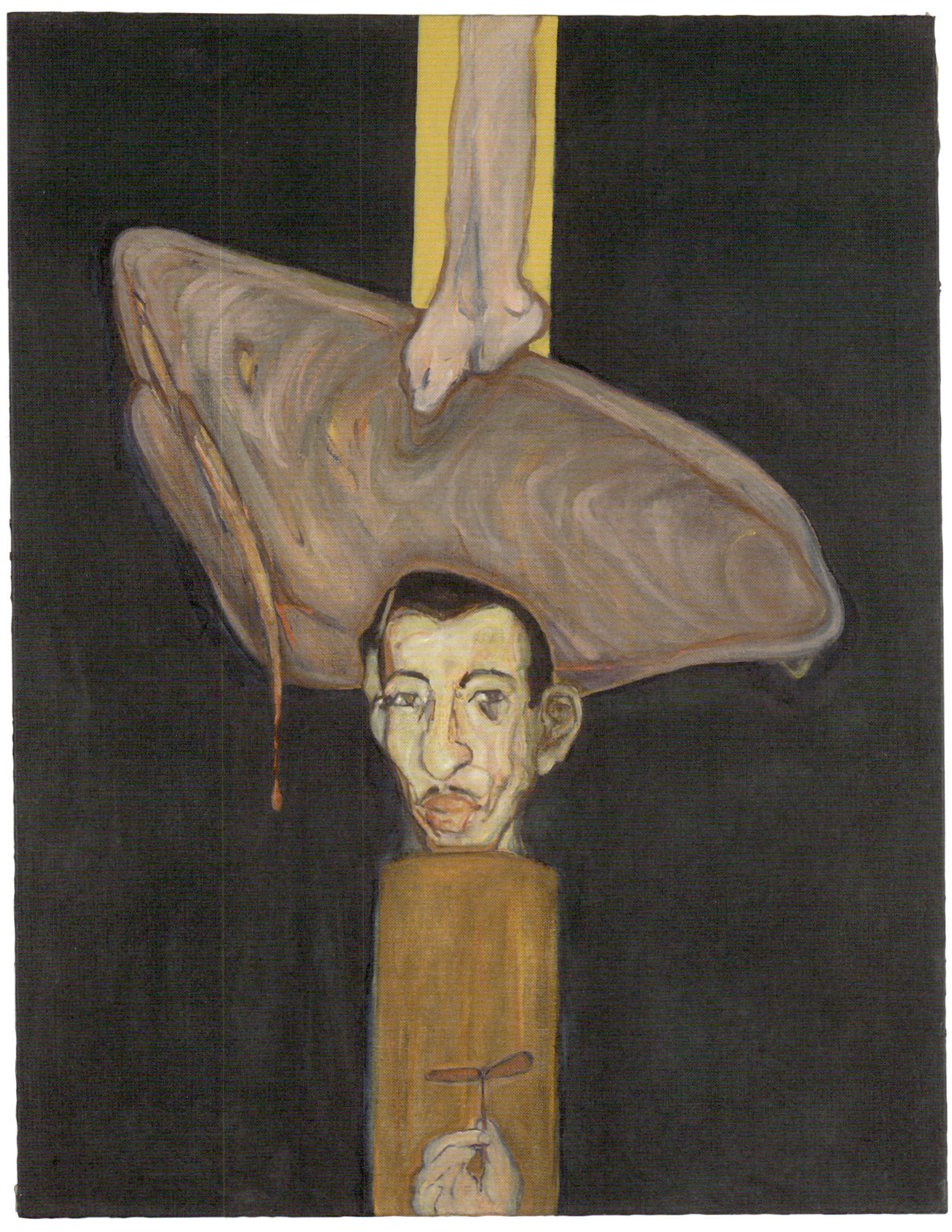

'I think utterly existentially … a painting is like a wound.'

– Marwan

Marwan
Bader Chaker al Sayyab 1965 Oil paint on canvas, 1300 × 975 mm
Tate, partial gift from the artist and partial purchase with funds provided by the
Middle East North Africa Acquisitions Committee 2016

Photography and Painting

As artists have responded to photography in their paintings, so too have a new generation of artists drawn from the traditions of painting in photography, using the photographic image to propose new ways of looking. Their spectacular large-scale photographs and precise compositions invite us to delve into the frame and explore collective experience, questioning social structures of representation and truth.

Artists such as Pushpamala N., Andreas Gursky and Louise Lawler manipulate their photographs in different ways to explore the constructed nature of image-making. They question what is a truthful representation of reality. Can an image convey the whole picture? Candida Höfer, Lawler and Thomas Struth show us that the way we present and arrange pictures determines what we perceive and how we experience them. How do we behave in a church or in a library, and, how do we therefore experience and understand artworks in these spaces? Does their significance and value change when shown discreetly on the floor, awaiting installation?

These works consider the act of looking: at images, at ourselves and at the world. In Struth's photographs, visitors gaze at paintings that, in turn, look at us. What are they seeing? Hiroshi Sugimoto's *Seascapes* capture the infinite: a universal image of the sea that has been encountered throughout generations. The series comprises 220 black-and-white photographs, developed over 30 years in different locations across the world. Somewhere between representation and abstraction, the works depict expansive views of the ocean against cloudless skies. They are punctured by a horizon line that cuts the compositions in half and delineates the limits of visual and mental perception.

The *Seascapes* convey the passing of time. Sugimoto refers to these works as 'time exposed', alluding to his technique of long exposure, whereby light gradually burns into the prints to produce an image. Unfolding endlessly beyond the horizon, Sugimoto's oceans position humanity in stark contrast to the vastness and persistence of nature. They ask us to reflect on the urgent need to protect our rapidly decaying planet – in Sugimoto's words, to 'think before destroying ourselves'.

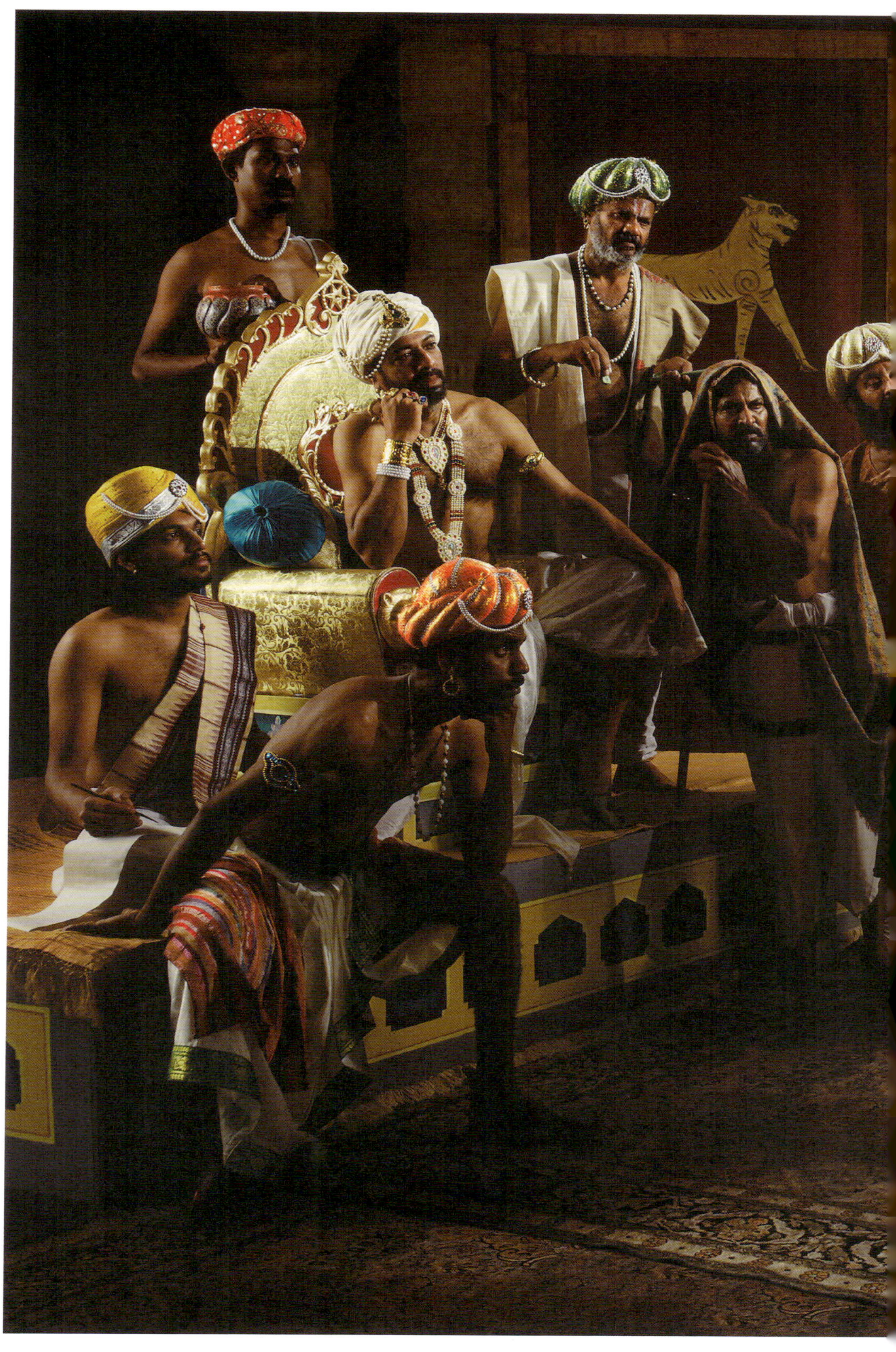

Pushpamala N. *The Arrival of Vasco de Gama (after an 1898 painting by José Veloso Salgado)* 2014
printed 2020 Inkjet print on canvas, 1426 × 2137 mm

Tate, purchased with funds provided by the Photography Acquisitions Committee and the South Asia Acquisitions Committee 2022

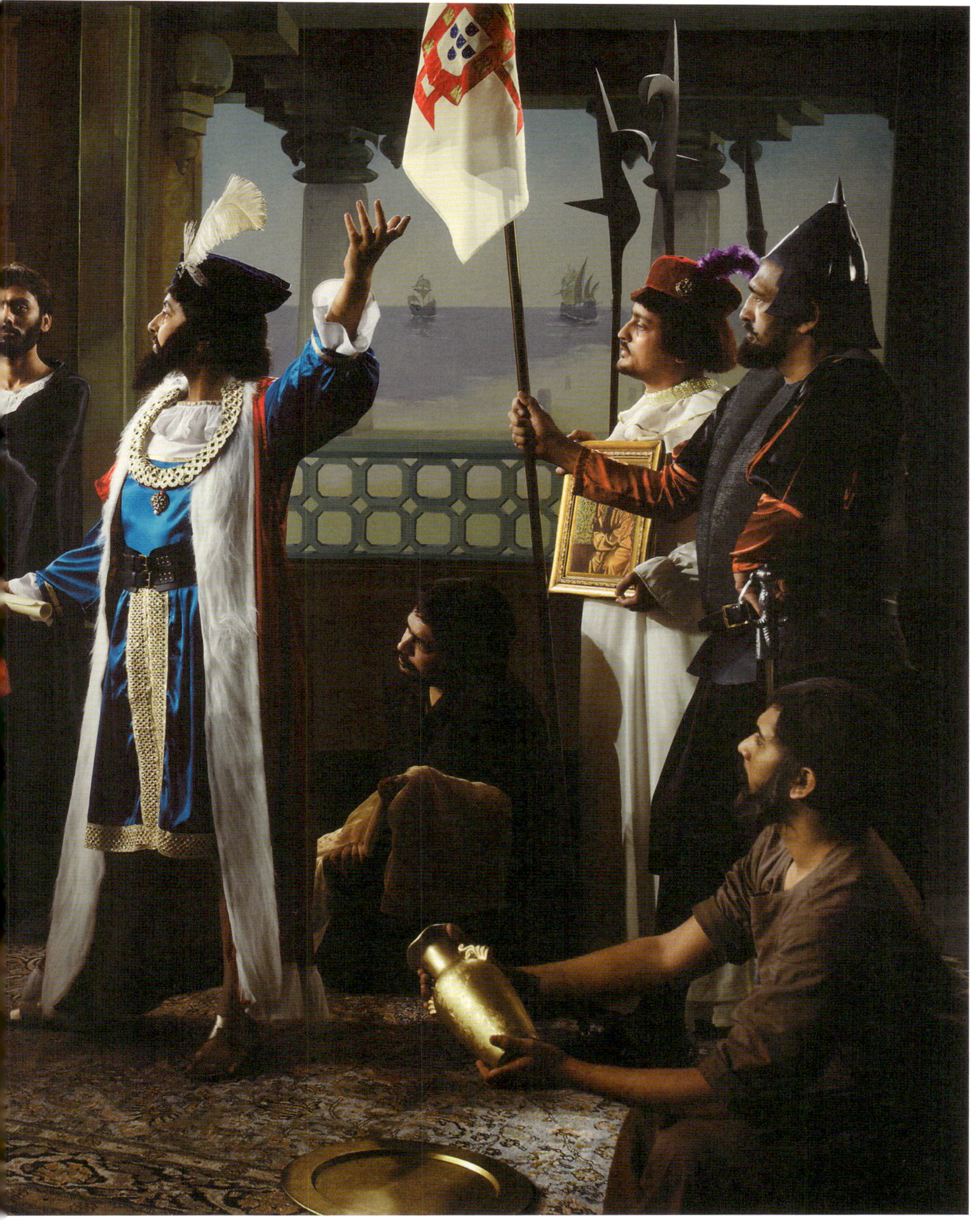

Dressing the Past
Pushpamala N.

I've been making masquerade works for some time now, but this was the first I made based on a history painting. My work is usually quite tongue-in-cheek and here I am: a woman playing a very macho, buccaneering character who was extremely cruel and ruthless. In fact, people often don't recognise it's me.

My picture is based on a painting made by José Veloso Salgado in 1898 to commemorate the 400th anniversary of Vasco da Gama's discovery of a sea route to India. The Portuguese explorer stands in the centre of the painting in front of the Zamorin, the King of Calicut, whose courtiers sit higgledy-piggledy all around him, wearing a mixture of costumes from different periods and geographies. It is supposed to be a history painting, but everything in it is wrong, historically. It's an illustration of a national myth.

Evidence was found later that the Zamorin refused to give Vasco da Gama an audience as the gifts he had brought were paltry. Also, another sailor – some say he was Arab, some say he was Gujarati – had helped him to cross the Arabian Sea from Malindi on the eastern coast of Africa to the Malabar Coast. He would never have reached India otherwise. This was the first step towards the colonisation and domination of India by European powers. While Vasco da Gama is known as a national hero in Portugal, today in India he is considered a pirate.

Usually, I take several months to produce a work, but I only had three weeks to make this one. I rented a large studio and rang up some friends. Everything is slightly off. We had to make the jewellery and the caps ourselves, and the Portuguese soldier's armour is made of a stiff buckram cloth. It's very DIY, which reminds people of school plays and having fun as kids dressing up.

Ten years later I'm still interested in this picture; it's still alive for me. My pose in the final picture isn't quite as strong as in some other versions, but it was late, and at least everyone has their eyes open.

'I am also interested in the idea of "cultural memory", and believe that by referring to these very familiar forms I can avoid the alienation of the viewer from art.'

– Pushpamala N.

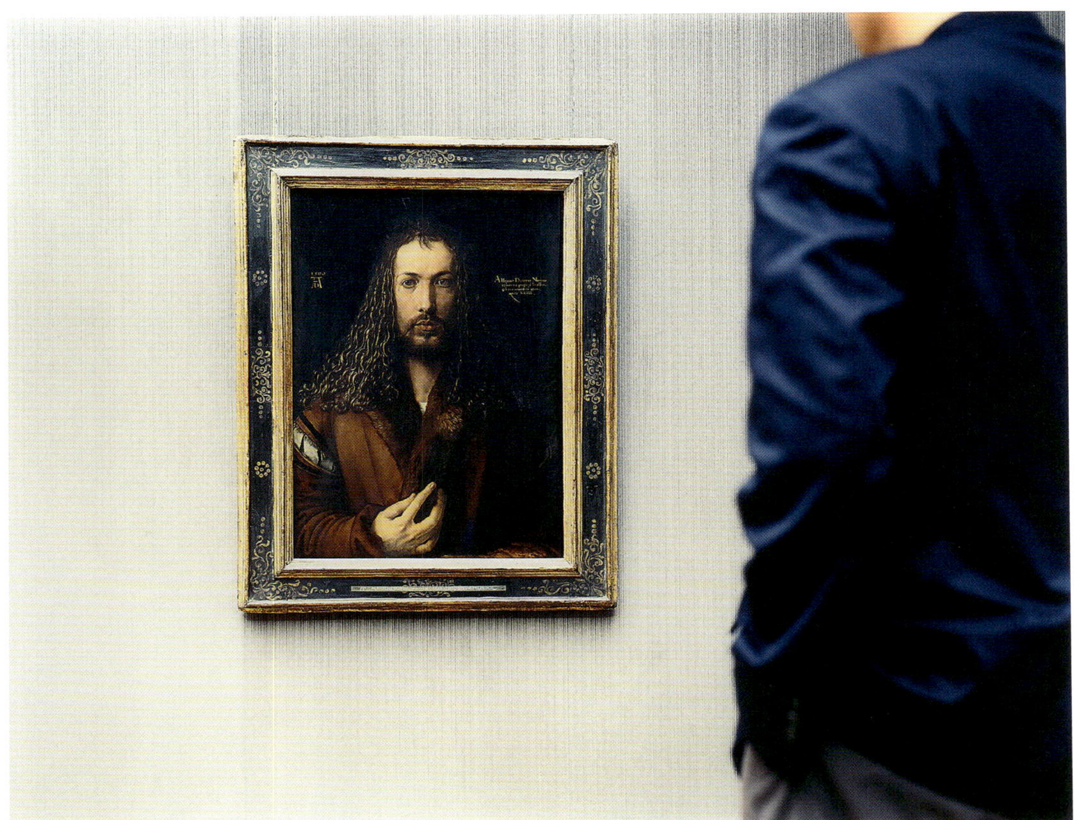

Thomas Struth
Alte Pinakothek, Self-Portrait 2000 Photograph, dye destruction print on paper, 1594 × 1873 mm
YAGEO Foundation Collection, Taiwan

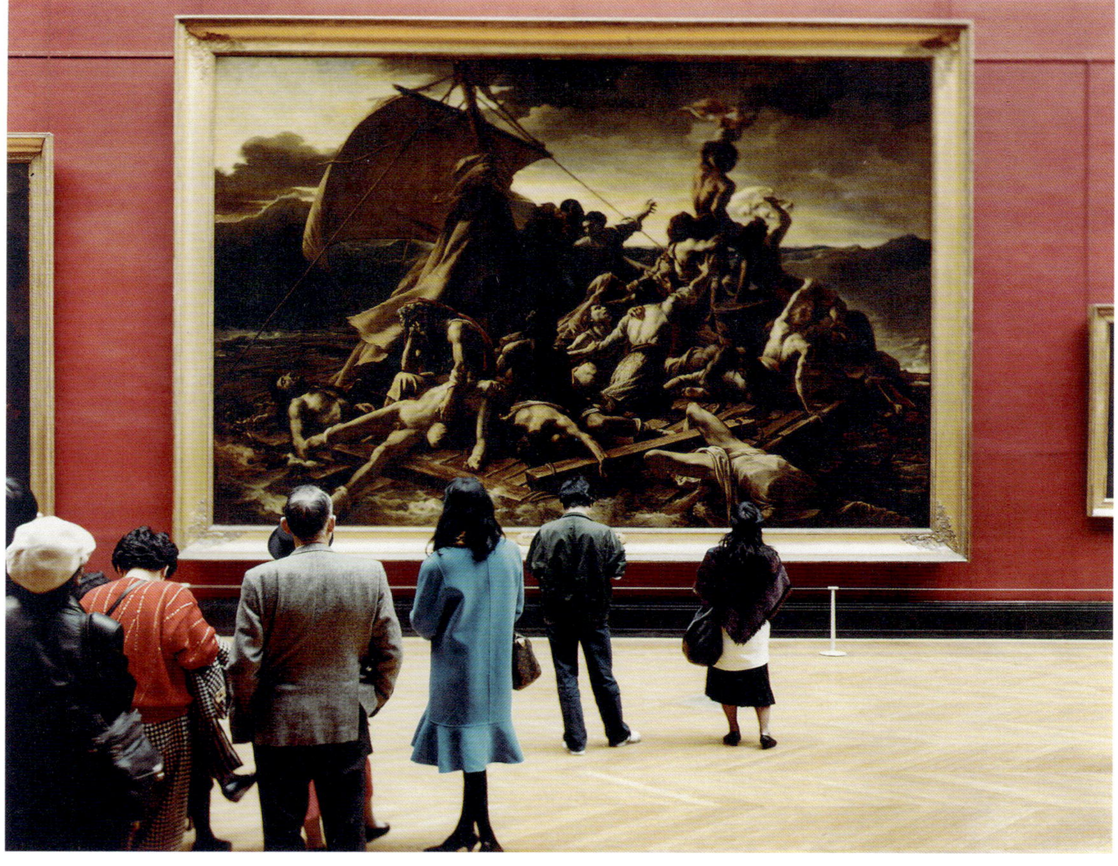

Thomas Struth
Musée du Louvre 1989 Chromogenic print on paper, 1835 × 2172 mm
YAGEO Foundation Collection, Taiwan

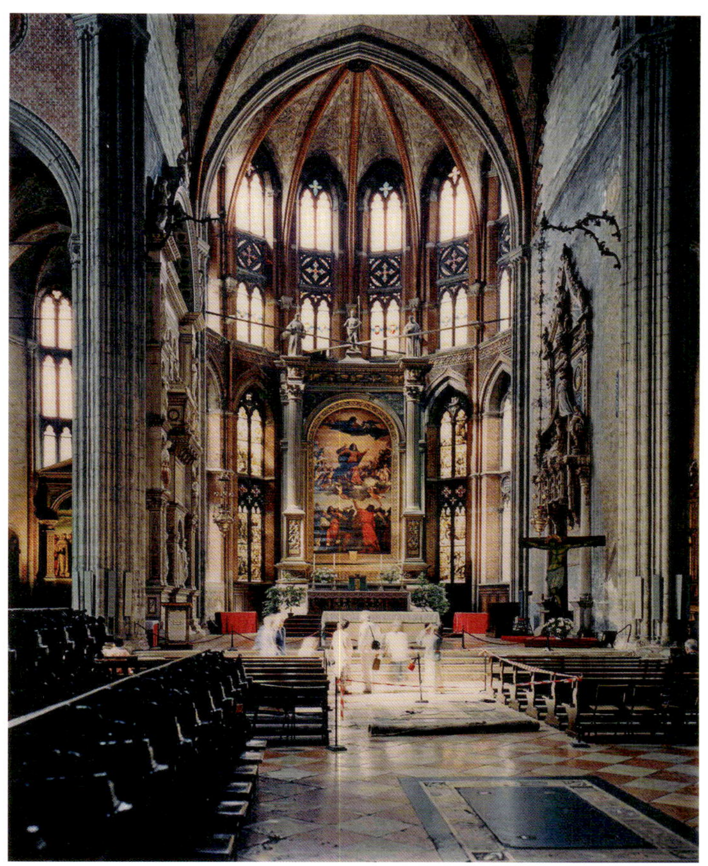

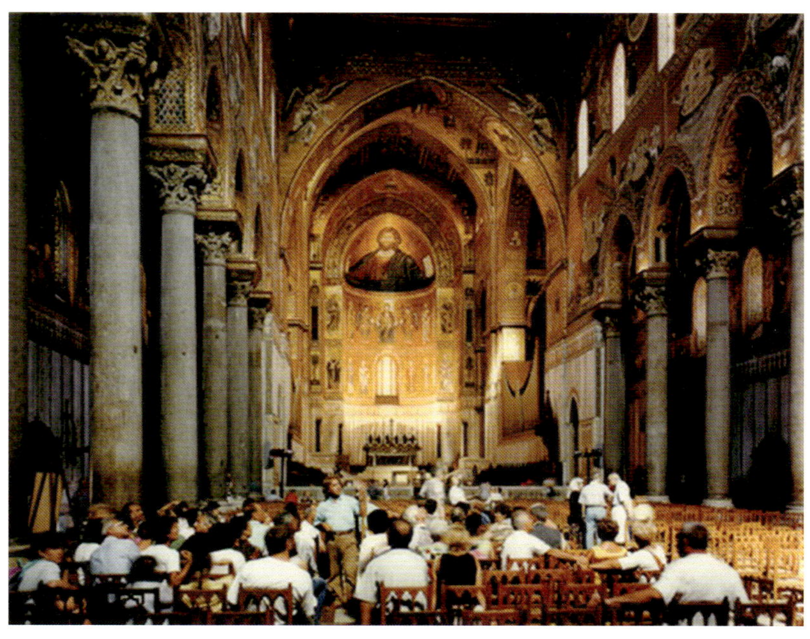

Chiesa dei Frari, Venice 1995 Cibachrome print, 2380 × 1880 × 50 mm
Basilica de Montreale, Palermo 1998 Colour coupler print, 1865 × 2315 mm
YAGEO Foundation Collection, Taiwan

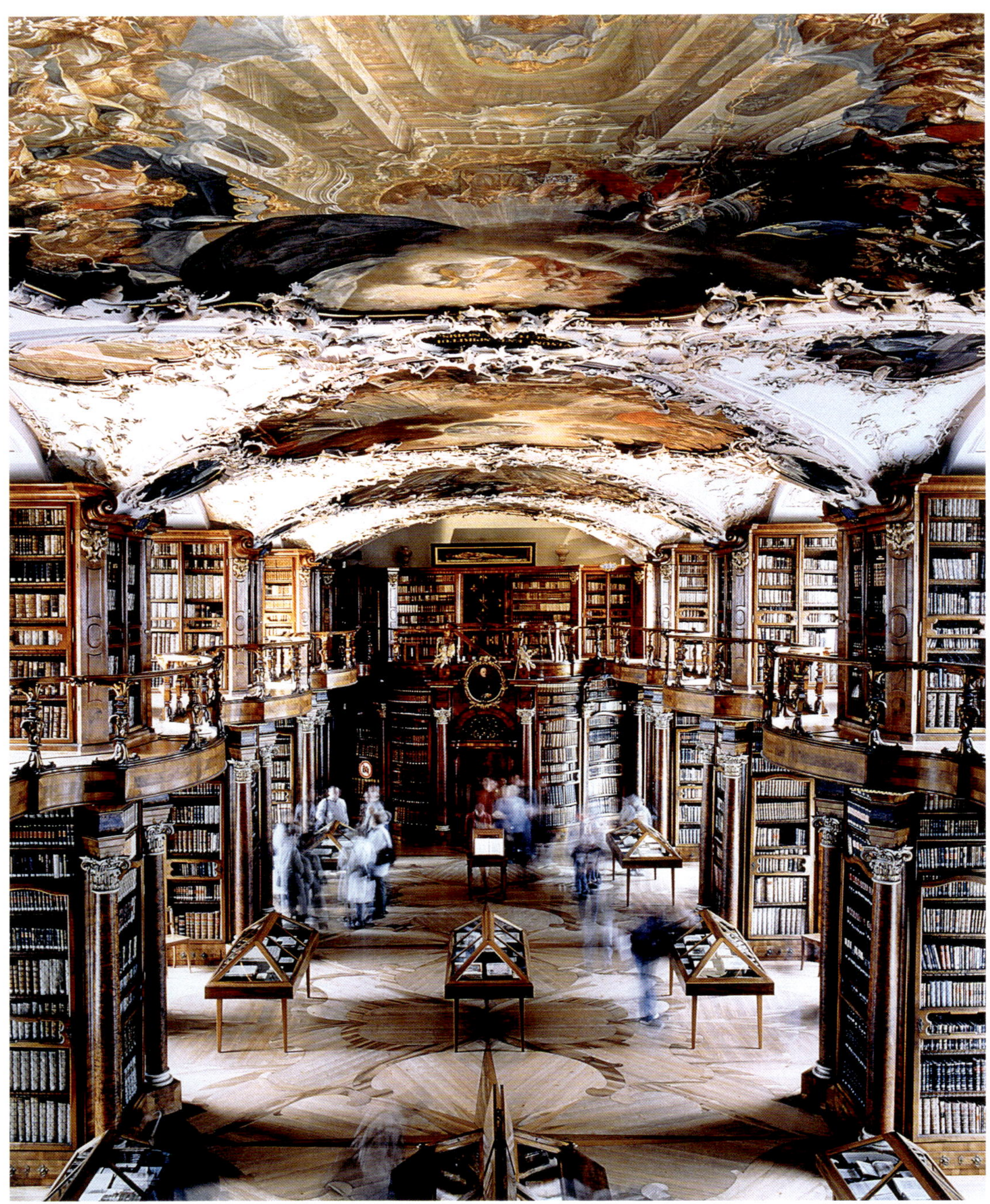

Candida Höfer
Siftsbibliothek St. Gallen I 2001 Photograph, colour, on paper, 1510 × 1210 mm

 Tate, purchased 2002

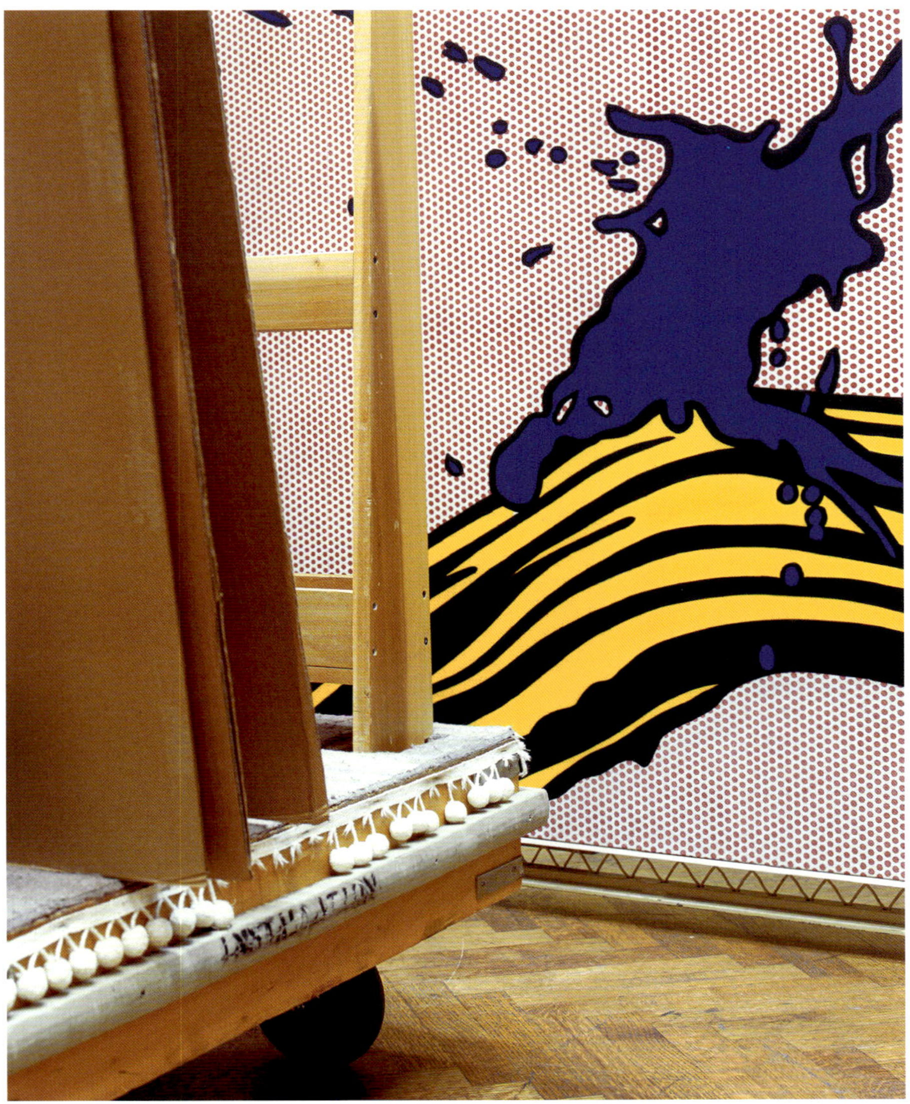

Louise Lawler
Splash 2006, printed 2012 Silver dye bleach print on museum box, 743 × 594 mm
Tate, purchased with assistance from the Karpidas Family (Tate Americas Foundation) 2013, accessioned 2021

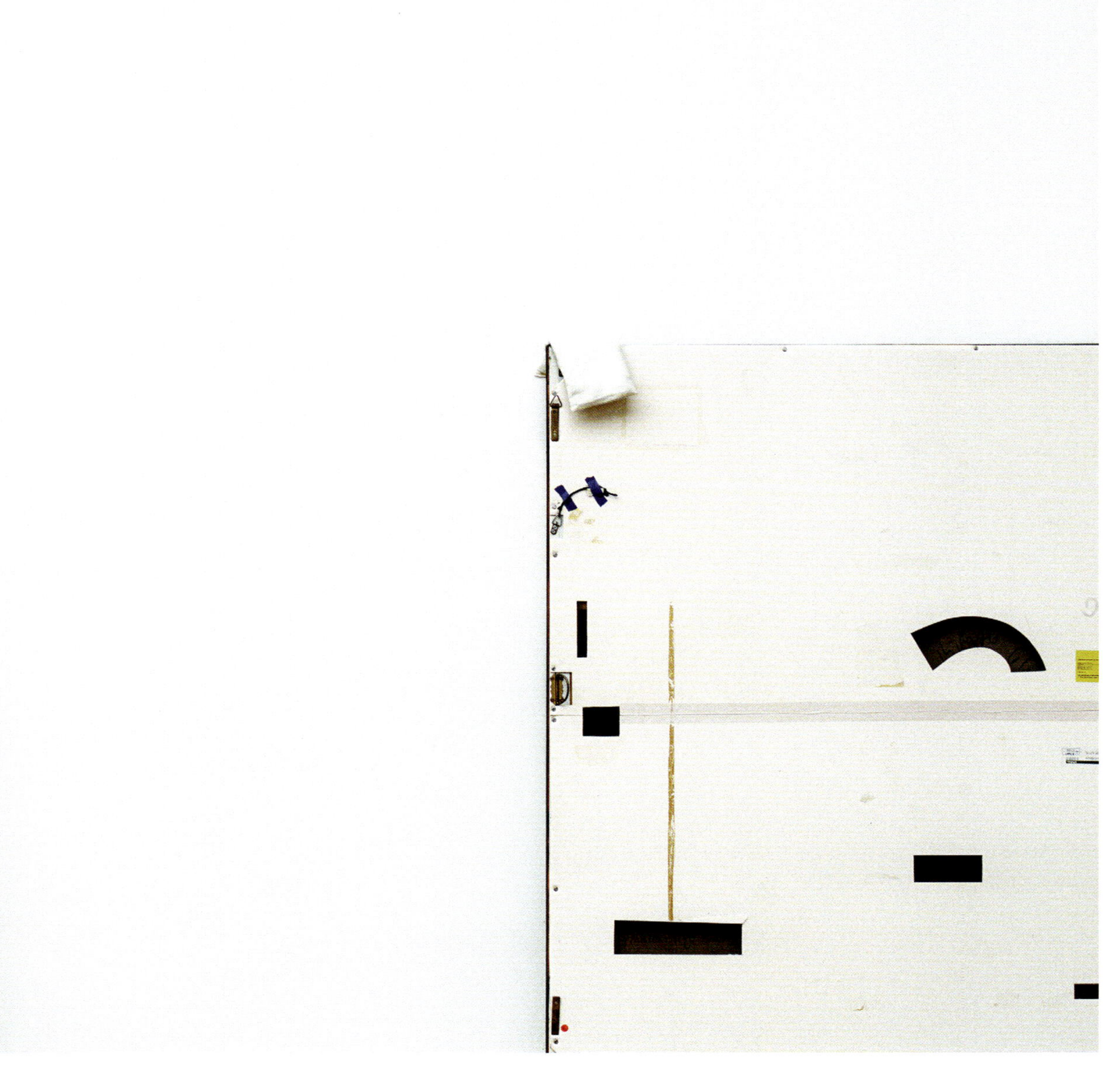

Louise Lawler
Wall Pillow 2010, printed 2012 Silver dye bleach print on museum box, 940 × 762 mm
Tate, purchased with assistance from the Karpidas Family (Tate Americas Foundation) 2013, accessioned 2021

'The effort of my work is to show
the habits and conventions of
looking at art by taking on aspects
of the system to make it visible.'
– Louise Lawler

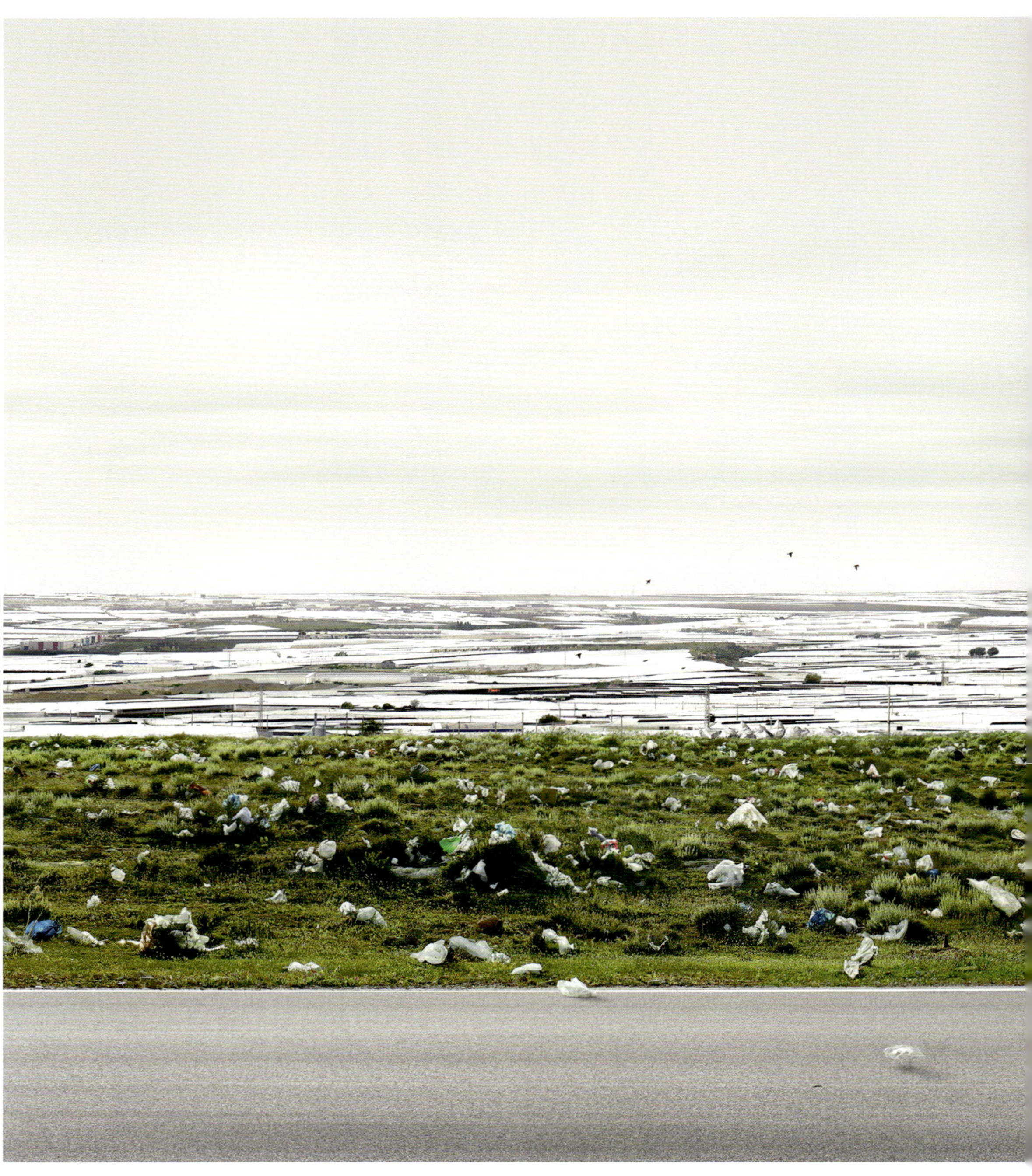

Andreas Gursky
El Ejido 2017 Photograph, inkjet print on paper, 2326 × 4076 × 64 mm

 YAGEO Foundation Collection, Taiwan

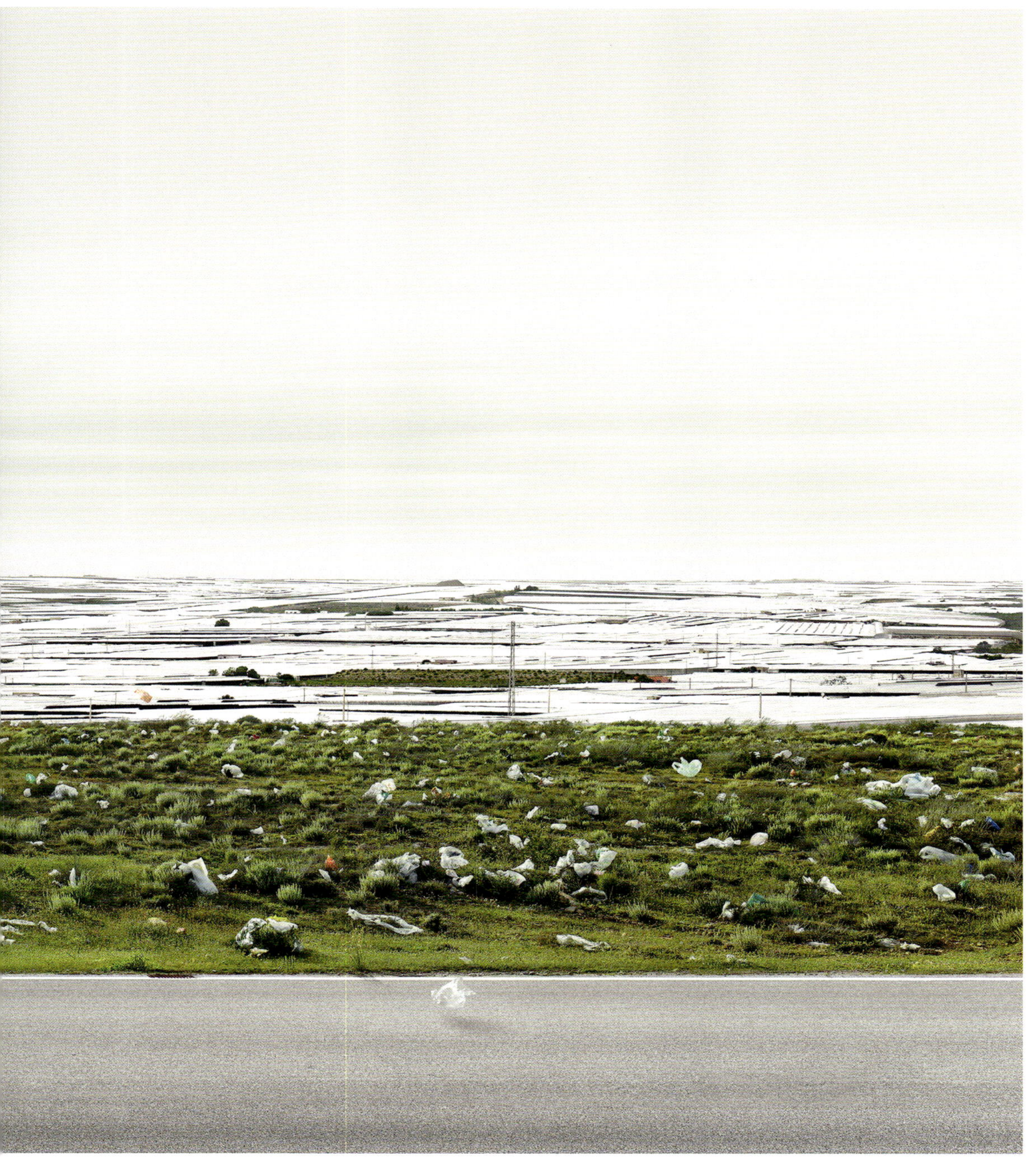

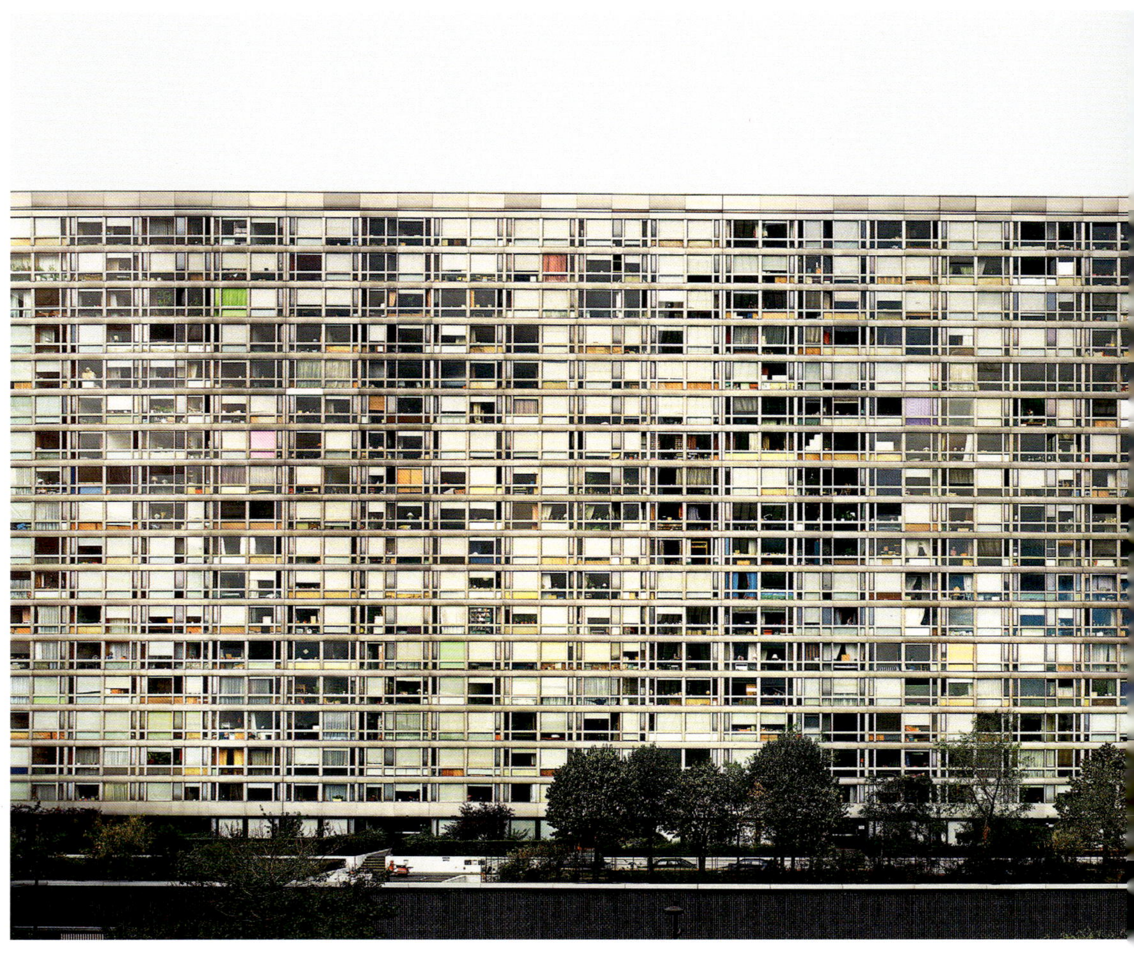

Andreas Gursky
Paris, Montparnasse 1993 Photograph, colour, on paper between glass and Perspex, 1342 × 3190 mm
Tate, purchased 1995

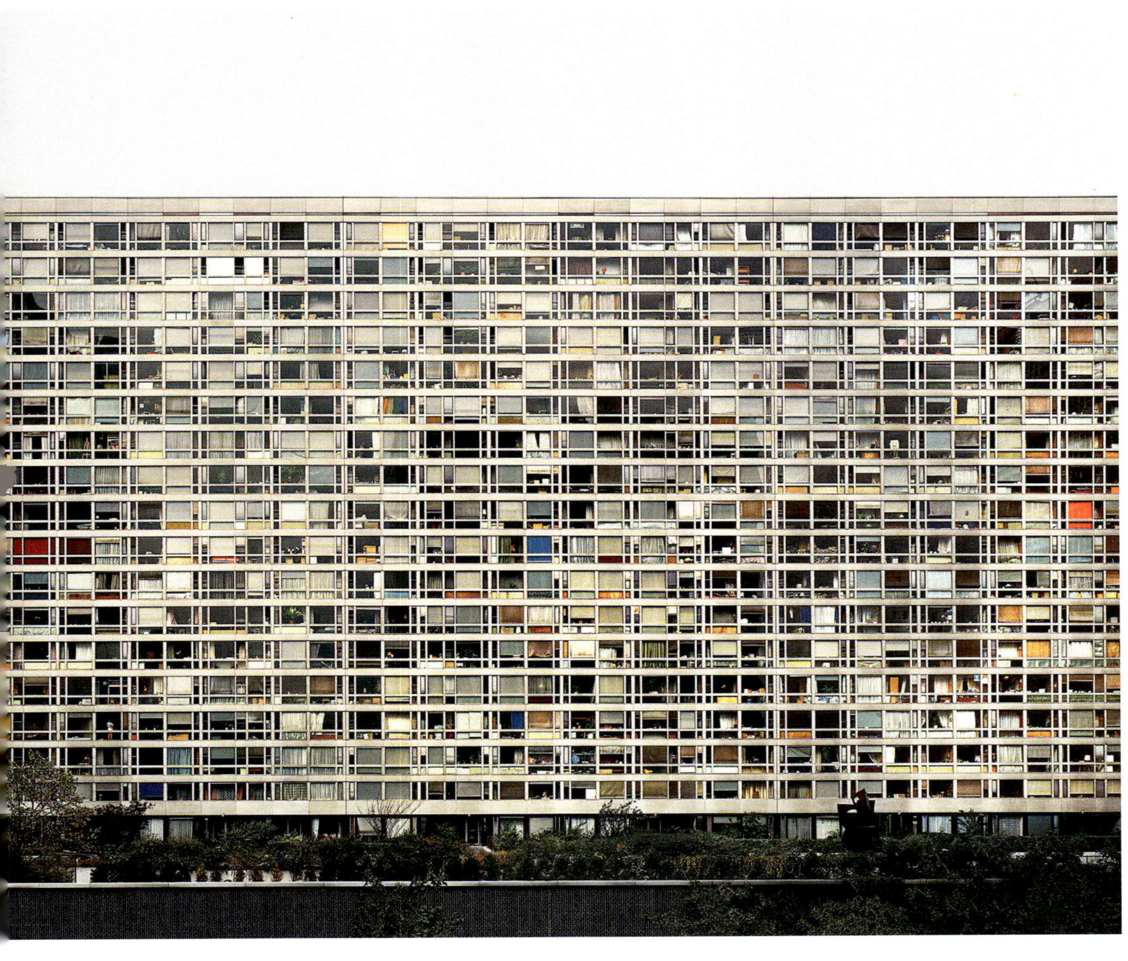

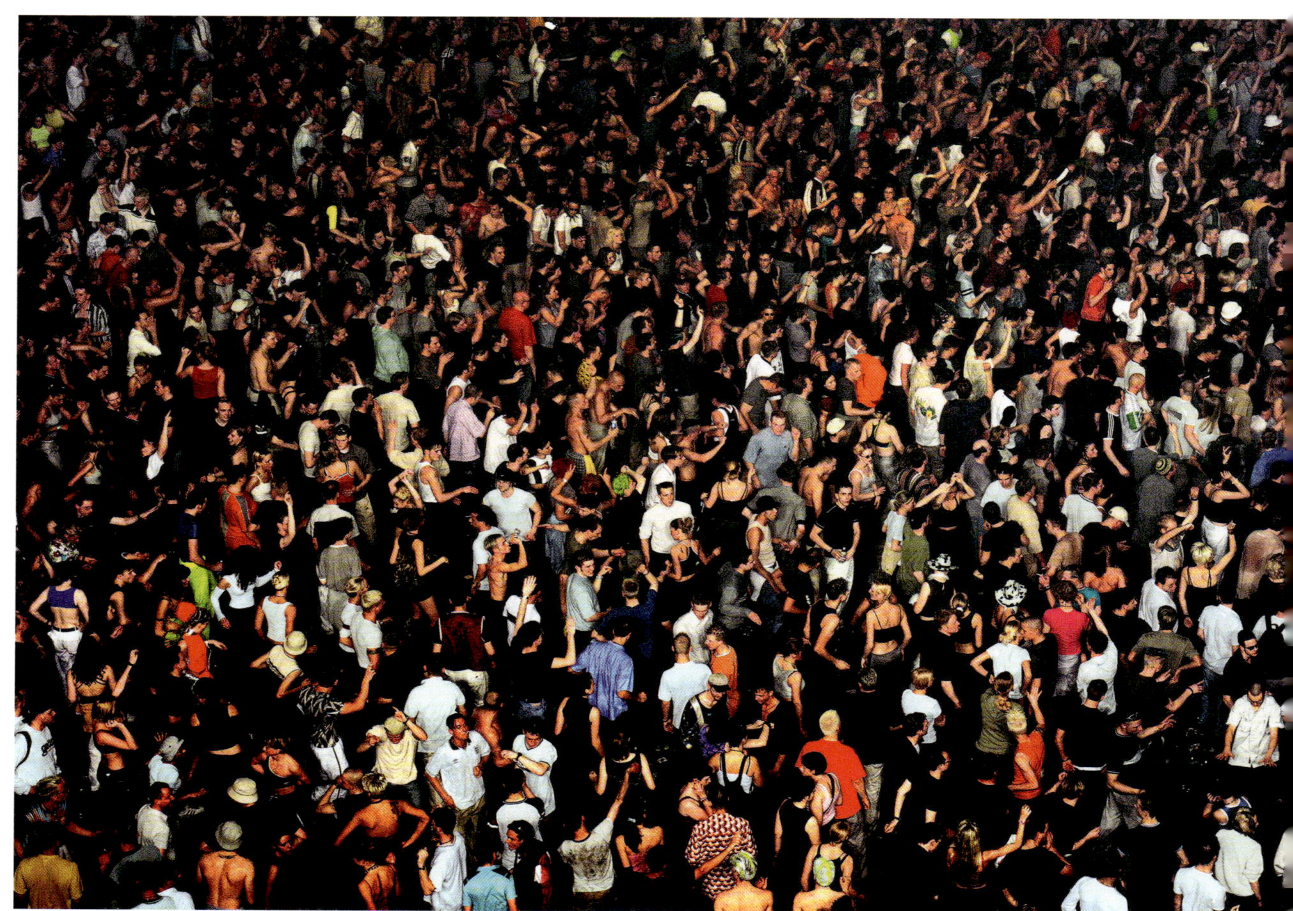

Andreas Gursky
May Day IV 2000 Photograph, C-print on paper, in artist's frame, 2083 × 5080 mm
  YAGEO Foundation Collection, Taiwan

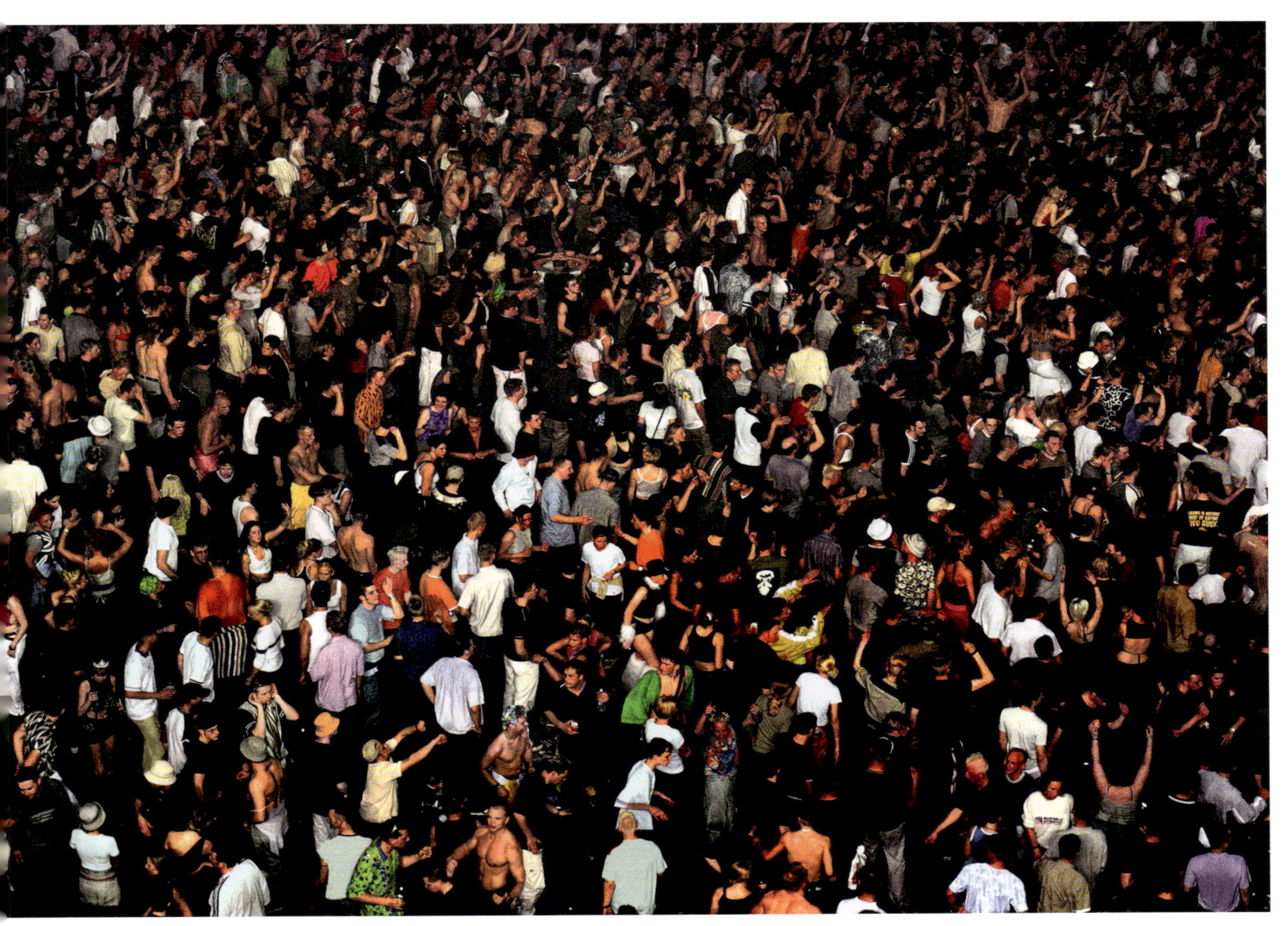

'Reality can only be shown by constructing it.'

– Andreas Gursky

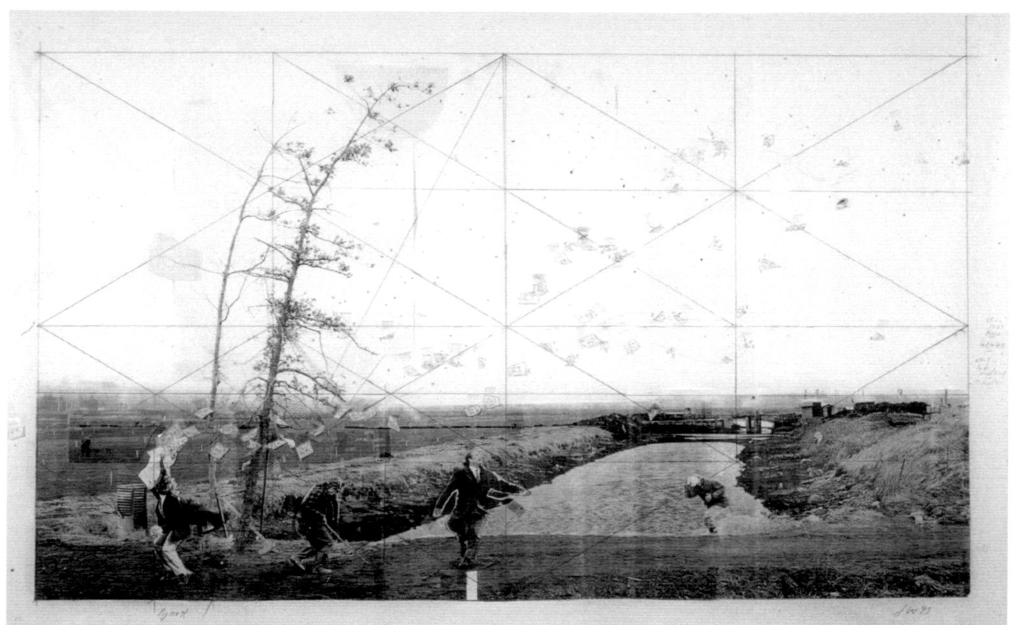

Jeff Wall
Study for 'A Sudden Gust of Wind (After Hokusai)' 1993 Printed paper and graphite on paper, 773 × 1215 mm
Tate, purchased 1997

On Jeff Wall

Beatriz Garcia-Velasco

Jeff Wall's work explores the boundary between truth and fiction, everyday life and fantasy, challenging the traditional notion that photography faithfully records reality. Wall initially trained as a painter and became interested in cinema, using large-scale photographs mounted on lightboxes as his signature medium. His work depicts landscapes and scenes of contemporary life, inviting viewers to unpick the entwining narratives of fleeting moments.

A Sudden Gust of Wind captures what seems like an instant frozen in time. It depicts four figures caught in a sudden gust that has swept across the open landscape. The photograph is, however, meticulously staged. The composition is based on a woodcut by Japanese painter and printmaker Katsushika Hokusai, and it took Wall over a year and more than a hundred separate shots to complete.

On windy days, Wall photographed actors in a landscape outside Vancouver. He then collaged and digitally superimposed elements of the images together. This analogue process is visible in *Study for 'A Sudden Gust of Wind (After Hokusai)'* (opposite). The study also reveals the careful placement of the sheets of paper blowing in the air. They act as a marker of the wind's direction and draw the viewer's gaze across the work, animating the scene.

There is no sense of connection between the figures; they appear to exist in different moments of time. Wall blurs the boundaries between movement and stillness. He weaves together the traditions of figurative painting with the technology of backlit photography and digital manipulation to play with the illusion of spontaneity. Wall often declares that he is indebted to historic art, particularly 'tableau' paintings, in which characters are staged for dramatic effect.

'Part of the poetry of traditional painting is the way it created an illusion that the painting depicted a single moment. In photography, there is always an actual moment – the moment the shutter is released. Photography was based in that sense of instantaneousness. Painting, on the other hand, created a complex and beautiful illusion of instantaneousness. So past, present and future were simultaneous in it, and play with each other or clash. Things which could never co-exist in the world could easily do so in a painting.'

– Jeff Wall

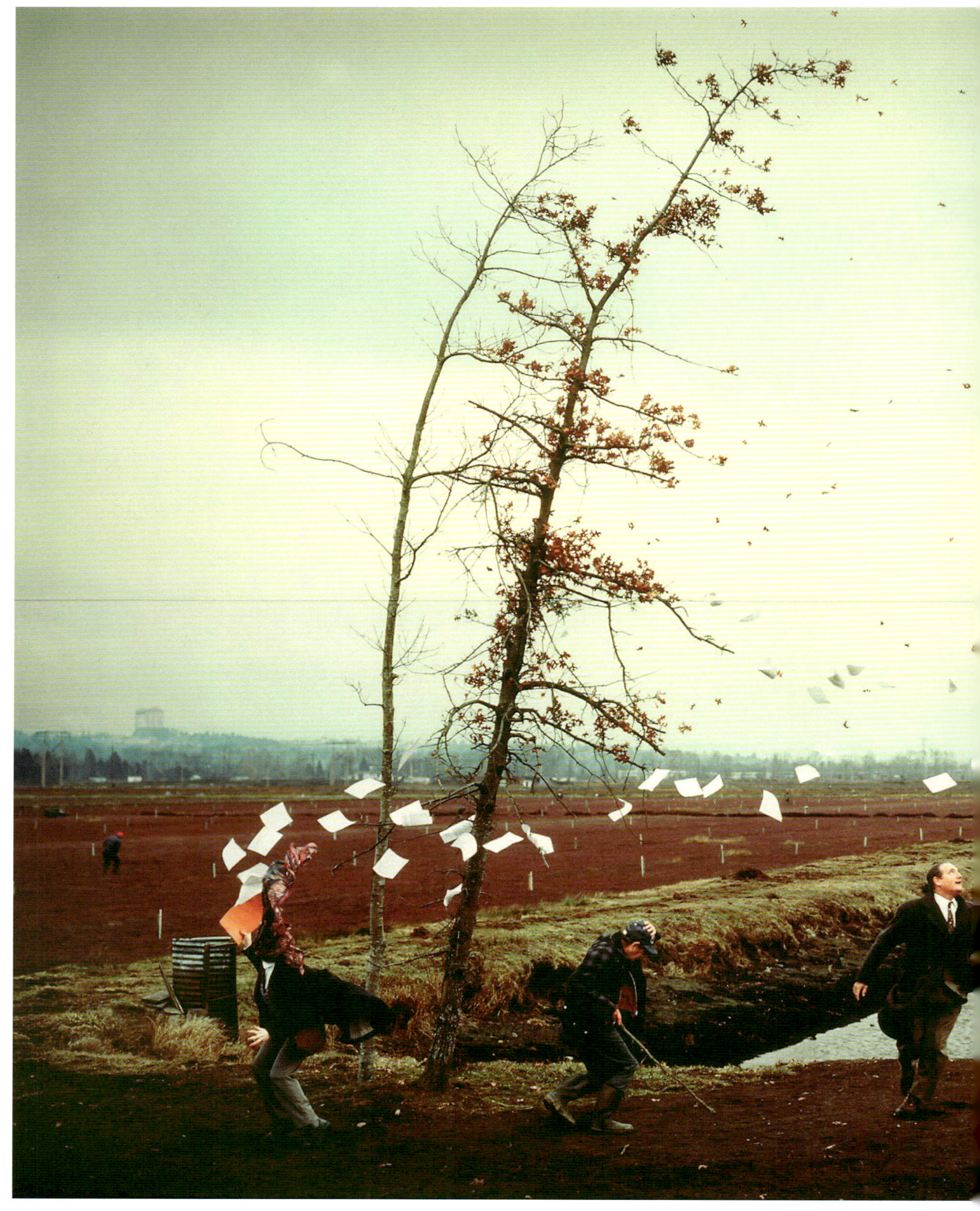

Jeff Wall
A Sudden Gust of Wind (After Hokusai) 1993 Transparency on lightbox, 2500 × 3970 × 340 mm

 Tate, purchased with assistance from the Patrons of New Art through the Tate Gallery Foundation and from the Art Fund 1995

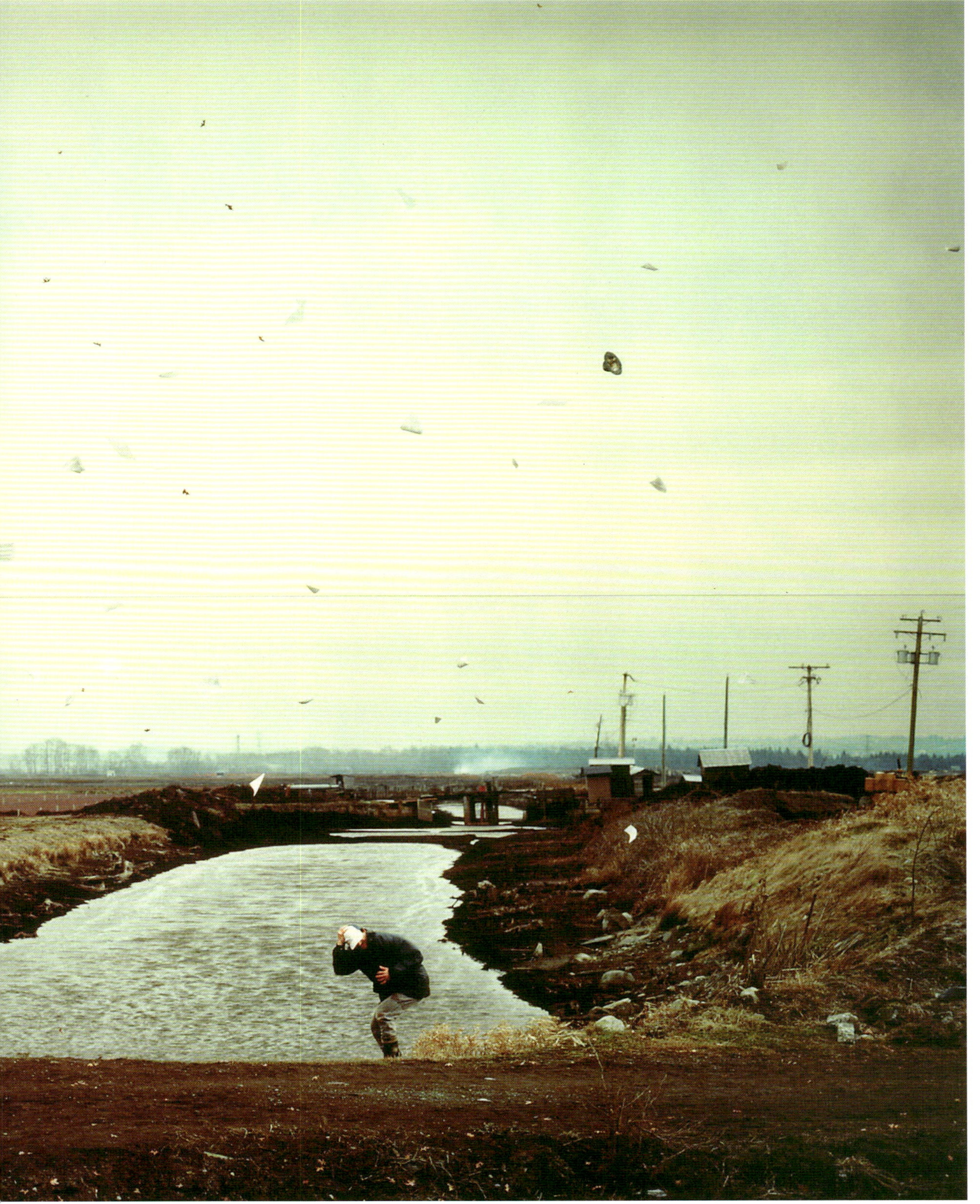

'Every time I view the sea, I feel a calming sense of security, as if visiting my ancestral home; I embark on a voyage of seeing.'

– Hiroshi Sugimoto

Hiroshi Sugimoto
Tyrrhenian Sea, Scilla 1993 Photograph, black and white, on paper, 422 × 542 mm
Tate, presented by the artist 1994

Hiroshi Sugimoto
Aegean Sea, Pilion 1990; *Tyrrhenian Sea, Scilla* 1993;
Ligurian Sea 1993; *Tyrrhenian Sea, Conca* 1994
Barry Schwabsky

Photographers often caption their images with the place and date – or sometimes just the year – when the shutter was released and the exposure made. The subject of the picture is not necessarily the named place and time. To take an example at random: a photograph by Lee Friedlander titled *Tokyo* and dated 1994. In it, I see nothing that reminds me of Tokyo. Instead, it shows a white man of a certain age wearing a V-neck T-shirt and a pair of eyeglasses hanging down on a neck strap; his eyes are closed as light pours in on his face from a window we don't see in an otherwise shadowy and nondescript room. This is, in fact, a self-portrait. But does it tell us any more about Friedlander than it does about Tokyo? I'd suggest it is something more like an allegory of photography itself – of the sightlessness that goes into its making something visible.

Hiroshi Sugimoto likewise designates his seascapes with a location and year, and they also turn out to be something like reflections on the nature of photography more than on their ostensible subjects. Here we have *Aegean Sea, Pilion* 1990, *Tyrrhenian Sea, Scilla* 1993, *Ligurian Sea* 1993 and *Tyrrhenian Sea, Conca* 1994. Each of them might almost be said to show next to nothing, just grey expanses, sometimes so faint as to seem like nothing more than a veil of fine ash or dust blown across the surface of the paper. And yet it's evident that each of these pictures presents a watery expanse beneath a vast sky. But the specificity of place suggested by those titles? It escapes me, no matter how hard I look. Identifying features are lacking. These scenes seem somehow placeless, as things might have been in the beginning, on the first day of creation, before the land had been made to separate the waters from the waters.

So, if these pictures are, as I think, no more about the places in their titles than Friedlander's Tokyo self-portrait is, then what are they about? Sugimoto's works often put a question mark on subject matter. Another of his series shows dioramas in natural history museums. The dioramas represent natural landscapes and the animals that inhabit them. But do the photographs depict what the dioramas depict, or do they depict the dioramas – or is the subject something else altogether? Again, one might think of photography itself as the subject: the way its images can blur the distinction between nature and artifice, reality and fiction. That blur is more cognitive than it is perceptual – more in the mind than the eye. Believing comes before seeing. Sugimoto reminds us to think twice before making a judgement. 'If you believe this scene is real,' he once said of one of his photographs, 'you have a problem in your eye'.[1]

That said, many of Sugimoto's photographs do feature a very evident blurriness, and among these are his seascapes. This blur is not just in the mind. It's right there in the print. It is the trace of time – of the unusually long period of exposure involved in making these pictures. Many photographers want to stop time, to extract from the transience of life a lasting token of that very transience. Sugimoto's seascapes don't do that. They offer an experience of duration. Everything transient – and what is more emblematic of transience than a wave? – has been, as it were, averaged out. All that is left is the above and the below and the border between them: sky and sea and, right through the middle of the composition, the horizon – a spatial division that may at times be stark (*Tyrrhenian Sea, Conca*), at others so evenly suffused with light as to become, in its 'ghostlier demarcations' (Wallace Stevens), nearly imperceptible (*Tyrrhenian Sea, Scilla*). While these four images happen to be linked to areas of the Mediterranean, Sugimoto has travelled all over the world to make his seascapes. Yet one has to wonder, did he really have to go so far to find these featureless skies and seas and horizons? Relations of light and shadow are distinct in each image, and yet one feels that the artist could merely have waited in one place and discovered as much variety through the ever-fluctuating weather, the inexorable movement of the sun through its daily arc and the change of seasons. Perhaps it's that he had to travel so much just to prove to himself that the sea is the sea everywhere.

Sugimoto once said that his earliest conscious memory is of a seascape: he was in a train emerging from a tunnel into the light by the sea. 'And the view made me feel, "I am here and I exist."'[2] Strange – encountering the sea, he did not observe that *it* exists but, in its presence, he felt his own existence. A vision of the sea was the ground of that feeling, and no wonder, for the sea was the origin of life. 'The Seascapes', Sugimoto said on another occasion, 'are before human beings and after human beings. The Seascapes were there before our presence, and when our civilisation is over, seascapes will still exist. Our presence is temporary'.[3] While many photographs preserve moments that are, in the scale of a human life, transient, these, by contrast, attempt to show something by comparison to which life reveals its transience.

This is one idea of what 'nature' means: what would be even if we were not. Considering those two contrasting statements of Sugimoto's, I have to wonder: are these ineffably subtle images meant to recall me to my existence, or on the contrary, to remind me of my once and future non-existence? I am tempted to imagine a synthesis; these works teach that our existence is a form of disappearance, and that the boundary between being and non-being is like the division between light and shadow – sometimes stark and incisive, more often faint and barely perceptible. Maybe the effect these images have on me as I contemplate them should be the mild vertigo of existential uncertainty. Is this somewhere or nowhere? Am I here or already gone? Perhaps these pictures are variable mirrors that reflect an absence: portraits of the absence of a subject.

Hiroshi Sugimoto
Aegen Sea, Pilion 1990 Photograph, black and white, on paper, 422 × 542 mm
Ligurian Sea 1993 Photograph, black and white, on paper, 422 × 542 mm
Tate, purchased 1994

Hiroshi Sugimoto
Tyrrhenian Sea, Conca 1994 Photograph, black and white, on paper, 1530 × 1824 mm
 YAGEO Foundation Collection, Taiwan

Capturing History

The photographic paintings of artists Gerhard Richter and Wilhelm Sasnal can be said to be pre-occupied with history, media and memory. In the act of copying or translating from photographic media to painted canvas, harmonies and contradictions emerge between the mediums. We tend to think of photographs as objective images, presenting an unbiased view of history. But does the clarity of the photographic lens obscure and distort as much as it reveals?

Richter grew up in post-war East Germany and his photopaintings are often concerned with histories of conflict, blending personal experience with this wider context. His landscapes are painted from photographs that Richter takes himself. They relate to nineteenth-century German Romantic painters, who saw themselves as mediators between divine nature and painted art. Richter takes the concept of mediation a step further, by painting a moment that has already been captured. This idea of artifice is also present in *Two Candles* 1982, which adopts the still-life tradition of *memento mori* – a reminder of death. The fleeting light of the candles is fixed forever as a painted image.

The photographs Sasnal paints from are taken from magazines, the internet and the ephemera of everyday life. Like Richter, he is interested in how painting can give photographic media a physical presence that somehow transforms the original subject.

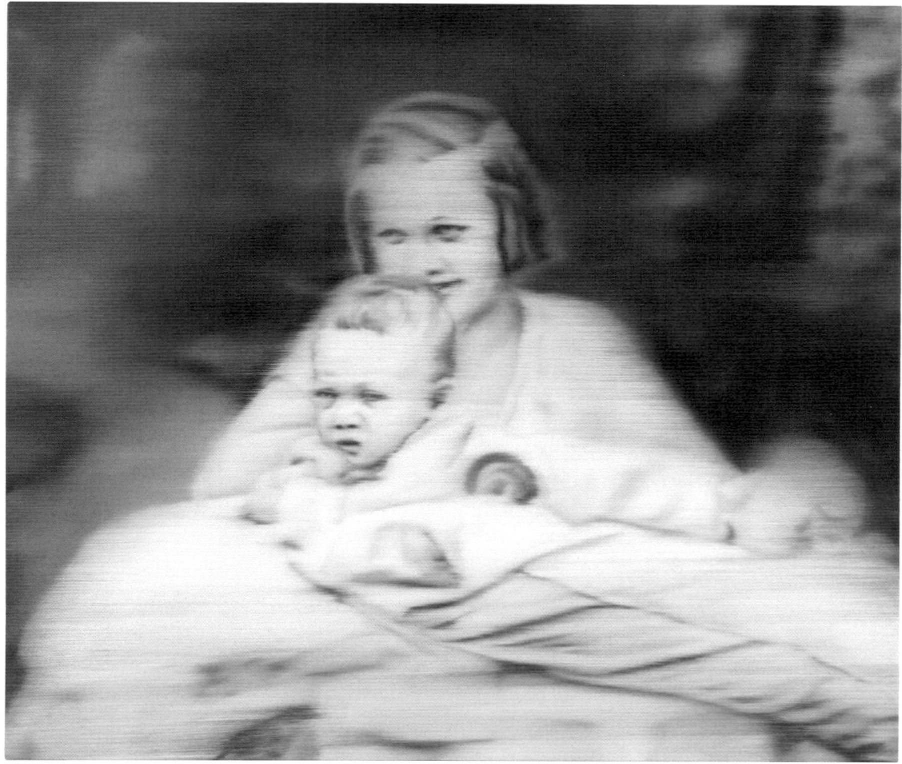

'The most banal amateur photograph is more beautiful than
the most beautiful painting by Cezanne.'

– Gerhard Richter

Gerhard Richter
Aunt Marianne 1965 Oil paint on canvas, 1200 × 1300 mm
YAGEO Foundation Collection, Taiwan

Iconography and Photography
An Interview with Gerhard Richter
Benjamin H. D. Buchloh

Benjamin H. D. Buchloh
Your photo painting of the early 1960s does have an anti-artistic quality; it negates individual handling, creativity, originality. So up to a point you do follow Duchamp and Warhol. And your painting also negates content, by demonstrating that the motifs are picked at random.

Gerhard Richter
But the motifs never were picked at random: not when you think of the endless trouble I took to find photographs that I could use.

So in every case the selection process was highly complex and explicitly motivated? So when I said in the Paris catalog that the choice of photographs was basically random, that was a highly questionable statement?

Maybe it was a good thing for it to look random.

So what were the criteria by which you chose photographs for your iconography?

Content, definitely – though I may have denied this at one time, by saying that it had nothing to do with content, because it was supposed to be all about copying a photograph and giving a demonstration of indifference.

And now the critics are trying to ascribe to you this iconographical concern with content. Ulrich Loock and Harten talk about a "death series": the airplane stands for death, the pyramid and the accident stand for death. To me it all seems rather forced, this attempt to construct a continuity for the death motif in your painting.

So you think I was looking for motifs that would be just a little bit shocking, while all the time I was totally indifferent to them?

I would agree, in that no selection can ever really be random. Every choice implies an attitude of sorts, however complex and unconscious. But, looking at your iconography in the 1960s, I find it very difficult to read into it a consistent theme of death. The Eight Student Nurses, *all right; but then there are the 48* Portraits. *It's irrational to read a death theme into those. What have the Chile paintings got to do with the pyramids? Or what have the townscapes to do with the mountain landscapes? The iconographical elements can all be connected, but not in the sense of a traditional iconography, where you say, "That's a death theme." To me it seems utterly absurd to try to construct a traditional iconography for your painting.*

Maybe it is just overdoing it a little to talk about a death theme. But as to whether the pictures have anything to do with death and pain, I think they have.

But this feature of content is not the determining, the decisive element in the selection.

That I don't know, and I can't really reconstruct my motives now. All I know is that there were reasons of content why I chose a particular photograph, and why I decided to depict this or that event.

In full awareness of the fact that content can no longer be conveyed through iconic depiction? So this is another contradiction: although you knew that – for example

– a death theme cannot be conveyed through straight depiction, you nevertheless tried to do just that, knowing full well that it was impossible.

For one thing, it isn't impossible at all. A picture with a dead dog in it shows a dead dog. It only gets difficult if you try to convey something above and beyond that, if the content gets too complex for straightforward depiction. But that doesn't mean that depiction can't convey anything.

Were you aware of the criteria by which you made your selection? How did you go about choosing the photographs?

I looked for photographs that showed my present life, the things that related to me. And I chose black-and-white photographs, because I realised that they showed all this more effectively than colour photographs, more directly, more inartistically, and therefore more credibly. That's why I picked all those amateur family pictures, those banal objects and snapshots.

What about the alpine pictures and the cityscapes?

Those were done when I no longer felt like doing figurative photo pictures, and wanted a change from the unequivocal statement, the legible and limited narrative. So I was attracted by those dead cities and Alps, which in both cases were stony wastes, arid stuff. It was an attempt to convey content of a more universal kind.

But if you really were concerned with that kind of content, how do you explain the fact that at the same time you brought nonfigurative painting into your work? The Color Charts, for instance, or other abstract paintings, done concurrently with the figurative ones. You were working on two levels at once, and this confused most of your critical commentators, who started to see you as a painter who knows all the tricks and techniques, and who simultaneously discredits and deploys all the

iconographical conventions. At the moment, this makes you particularly attractive to many viewers, because your work looks like a survey of the whole universe of twentieth-century painting, presented in one vast, cynical retrospective.

Now that definitely is a misunderstanding. I see no cynicism or trickery or guile in any of this. On the contrary, it all seems rather amateurish to me, the head-on way I've tackled everything, and how simple it is to read off what I had in mind and what I was trying to do. That's why I don't really know what you mean by the contradiction between figurative and abstract painting.

Let me take Table *as an example, one of your earliest paintings.* Table *already has both elements within it: a totally abstract, gestural, self-reflective quality on one hand and on the other the function of depiction. And this is surely one of the great twentieth-century dilemmas: this apparent conflict, this apparent antagonism within painting between the functions of depiction and self-reflection. In your painting, the two run very close together. But aren't they juxtaposed in order to show up the inadequacy, the bankruptcy of both?*

Not bankruptcy, but always inadequacy.

Inadequacy in relation to what? The expressive function?

In relation to what is expected of painting.

Can that expectation be formulated?

That painting ought to have more effect.

So you would reject the accusation that is so often leveled at you, of cynical complicity with painting's lack of effect?

Yes, I would, because I do know that painting is not without an effect – I only want it to have more of one.

So the simultaneous pursuit of depiction and self-reflection has nothing to do with the two cancelling each other out; and you are just using different means to give substance to what is expected of painting?

Yes, more or less.

So, in the early 1960s you don't see yourself as the heir to a historical dichotomy, a state of fragmentation, in which no strategy is really valid anymore?

I do see myself as the heir to a vast, great, rich culture of painting – of art in general – which we have lost, but which places obligations on us. And it is no easy matter to avoid either harking back to the past or (equally bad) giving up altogether and sliding into decadence.

Which brings you, of course, to the brink of a political argument, which maybe you don't relish. But how would you explain this loss, if not in terms of politics, or social history, or just plain history? The way you put it, it almost sounds like Adorno's famous statement that "After Auschwitz, lyric poetry is no longer possible." Does that ring true for you?

No. There is lyric poetry after Auschwitz.

When you say that no one can paint that way anymore –

By that I meant first and foremost a specific quality that we have lost.

How?

Photography is certainly one external factor involved in the fact that we've forgotten one way of painting and can no longer produce a certain artistic quality.

It can also be put in entirely functional terms, by saying that – among other things – paintings have lost their descriptive and illustrative functions because

photography has assumed those functions so perfectly. The result is that the job is no longer there to be done, and the high artistic quality of old paintings, which you mention, has its material and historical roots partly in those very same descriptive and illustrative functions.

The quality can't be entirely explained away in terms of the illustrative function. All that perfection of execution, composition and so forth would still have been lost to us, even if there had never been such a thing as photography. Literature and music are in the very same mess. People praise Mozart and Glenn Gould to the skies, because the new composers can't offer the same thing anymore, even though music hasn't been edged out by anything analogous to photography.

So if the loss doesn't stem from the evolution of reproductive technology, or from the experience of previously undreamed-of historical catastrophes (as Adorno suggests in the sentence I quoted), or from the destruction of bourgeois culture, or from political factors of any kind – and you've rejected all those, at least in passing, as explanations –

No, they all play their part, but I see the basic fact as the loss of the Centre.

In Sedlmayr's sense? You can't be serious?

Yes, I am; what he was saying was absolutely right. He just drew the wrong conclusions, that's all. He wanted to reconstruct the Centre that had been lost.

And to reconstruct the Centre by using methods and means that were entirely incapable of achieving it. But how do you describe it, if it's so obvious to you?

I've no desire to reconstruct it.

No, but you must be able to describe it. And then it's a historical process after all –

Yes, but there are specific, new, concrete facts which have altered our consciousness and our society, which have overturned religion and therefore changed the functioning of the State. There are only a few makeshift conventions left to regulate the thing, keep it practicable. Otherwise there's nothing there anymore.

Is painting one of those conventions?

No. The criteria of painting are conventions – and harmful ones, because they are ideologically defined. They block enlightenment. That's why I think so highly of psychoanalysis, because it takes away prejudices and turns us into responsible adults, autonomous beings who can act more rightly and more humanely in the absence of authorities, or God, or ideology. So it's a good thing to lose all that.

And you'd want the same for painting?

Yes.

So on one hand you see the process as irreversible, and above all impossible to reconstruct by cultural means –

That would only serve to delay it.

And political means seem to you at best problematic or questionable, or not directly applicable.

Politics operates more by faith than by enlightenment, so nothing is going to come of that.

But you see the role of art as a more important one than that of simply liquidating a false bourgeois cultural inheritance – though that is one of its functions, isn't it?

Liquidating? Yes, that's part of it.

But at the same time it also has another function, and that's where the contradiction comes in. What is the other function, if not a political one?

Above all, art does more than destroy. It produces something, a different image.

Of autonomy?

Yes.

And how is the painted picture supposed to constitute a model of that autonomy, here and now?

The painting is *one* important, possible way among others, one that can be used. At worst, it's on offer to those who are interested.

About your self-imposed limitation to the practice of painting – when it comes to liquidating the bourgeois inheritance while constructing the new autonomy, isn't that limitation rather a handicap? Shouldn't we suppose that there are other and more radical ways and means that will carry out the liquidation more quickly and thus also make anticipation more fruitful?

No, in this respect I'm extremely conservative. It seems to me like someone saying that language is no longer usable, because it is a bourgeois inheritance, or that we mustn't print texts in books anymore but on cups or on chair legs. I am bourgeois enough to go on eating with a knife and fork, just as I paint in oil on canvas.

So, all attempts to pursue one side of the dialectic more rapidly by artistic means seem to you to be unacceptable. Would you retrospectively criticise Duchamp, who gave up painting for this very reason?

I'm not sure that those were his reasons. But you can never take that as a sufficient reason to give up painting. To interpret Duchamp in that way, and go in for politics and criticism instead, is pathetic.

Pathetic in what way? In terms of painting's liquidation of bourgeois culture, or in terms of its capacity for anticipation?

Because it achieves nothing. It's neither artistic nor political action. It's amateur.

To put it in specific terms: would you regard it as a premise of your present-day painting that it remains in the very dilemma you faced from the start: that is, to play off the real facts of mass culture, as you see them in photography, against the esoteric and elitist conditions of high culture, in which you as an artist have a part? And that you base your work on this dialectic, assuming yourself to be exempt from the contradiction; and that in practice there is no solution that you can accept? Is this still a premise, or did it apply only to the 1960s?

I see no such premise, then or now.

But your quoted statement on Cézanne says exactly that. When you say, "I consider many amateur photographs better than the best Cézanne", that seems to express this very contradiction.

Yes, but that doesn't mean that I could ever change anything directly through painting. And it certainly doesn't mean that I could do it without painting.

Why have you so firmly rejected any concrete political intention in your own art?

Because politics don't suit me, because art has an entirely different function, because all I can do is paint. Call it conservative.

But by limiting yourself to the medium of painting, mightn't you be espousing not just a conservative

position but maybe also a critical dimension? Are you, for instance, calling into question the immediacy claimed by work like that of [Joseph] Beuys?

Naturally, by limiting myself to painting I imply a criticism of a lot of things that I don't like, not all of them connected with painting.

So you don't deny on principle that someone might validly intend to make a critical political statement through art?

I probably do deny it. But what counts is that I have to take as my starting point, my foundation, my own possibilities and my own premises.

And you say that these are unchangeable –

Largely unchangeable.

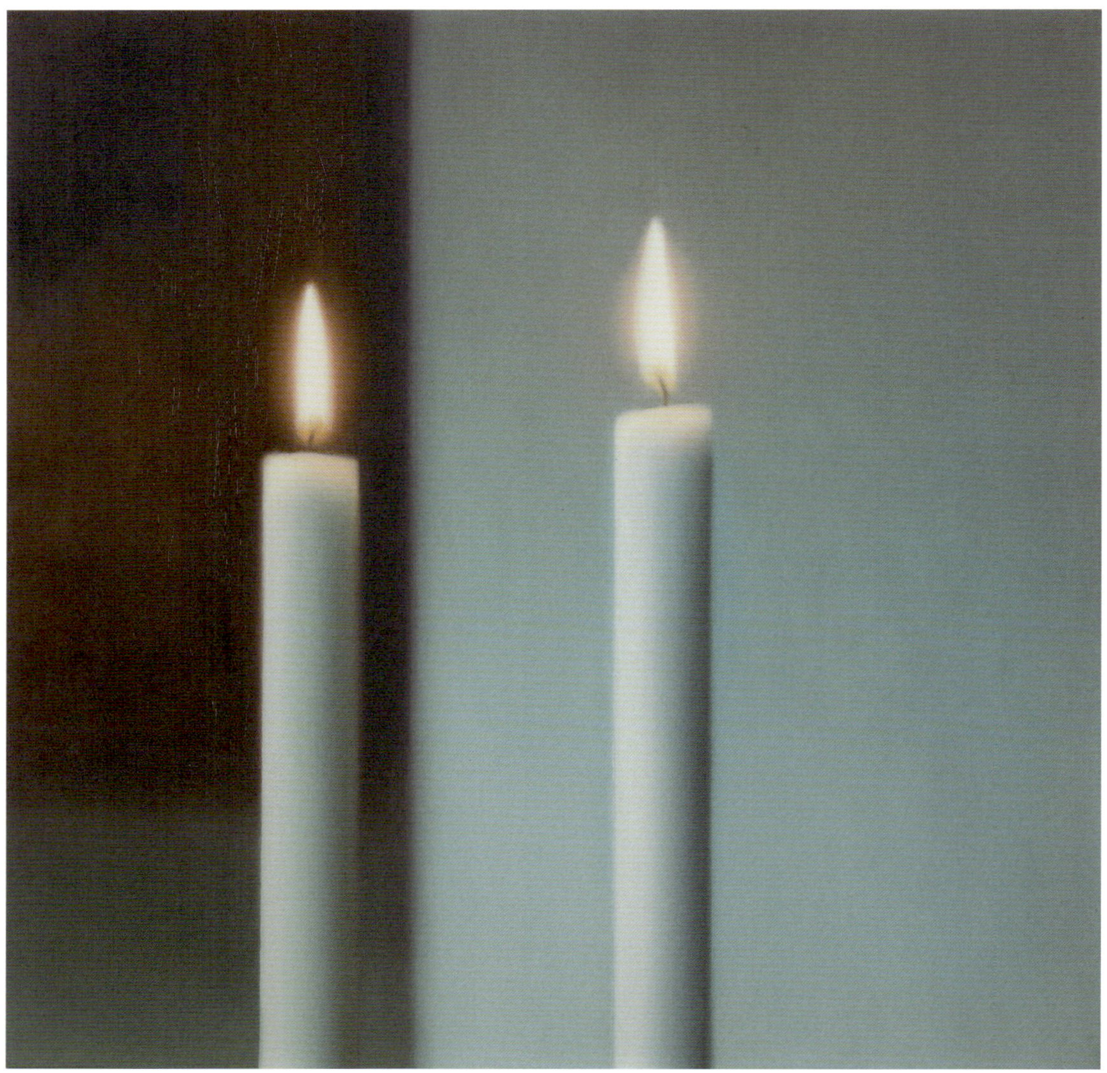

Gerhard Richter
Two Candles 1982 Oil paint on canvas, 1400 × 1400 mm
YAGEO Foundation Collection, Taiwan

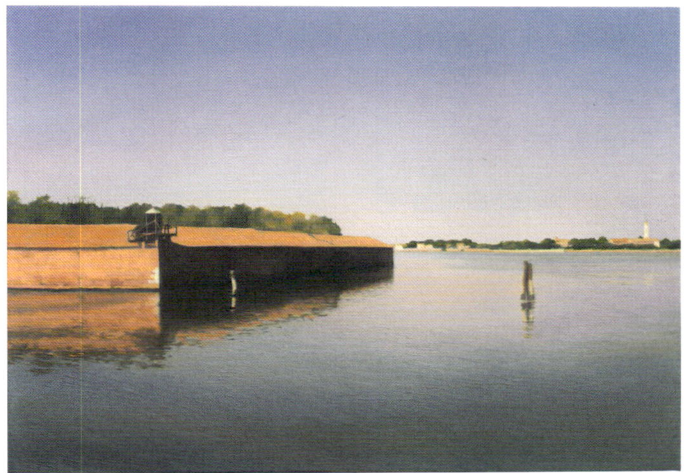

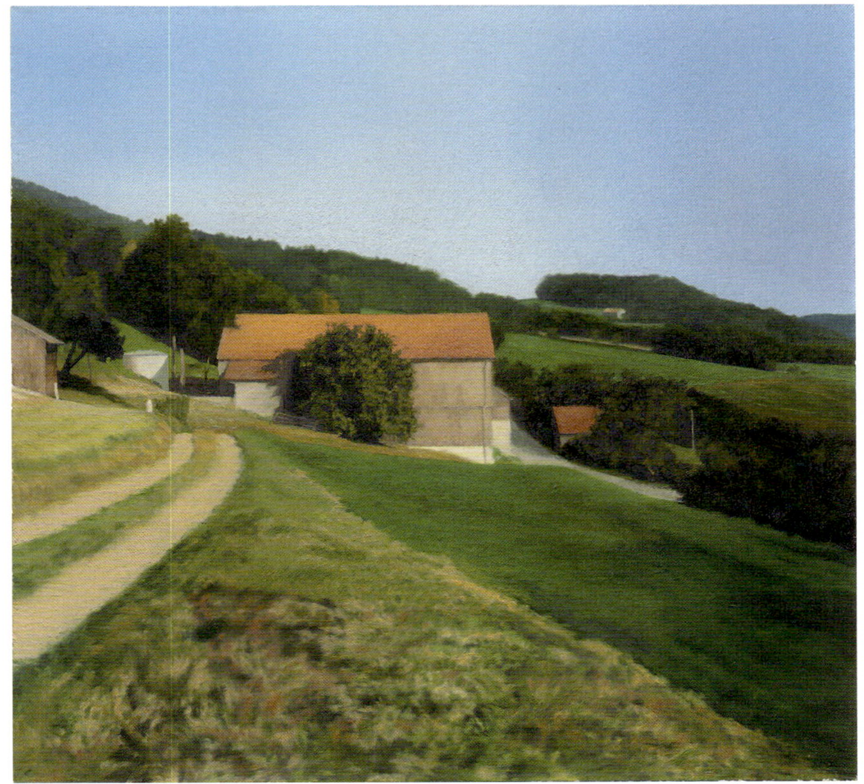

Venice (Island) / Venedig (Insel) 1985 Oil paint on canvas, 504 × 700 mm
Barn (Scheune) 1984 Oil paint on canvas, 950 × 1000 mm
YAGEO Foundation Collection, Taiwan

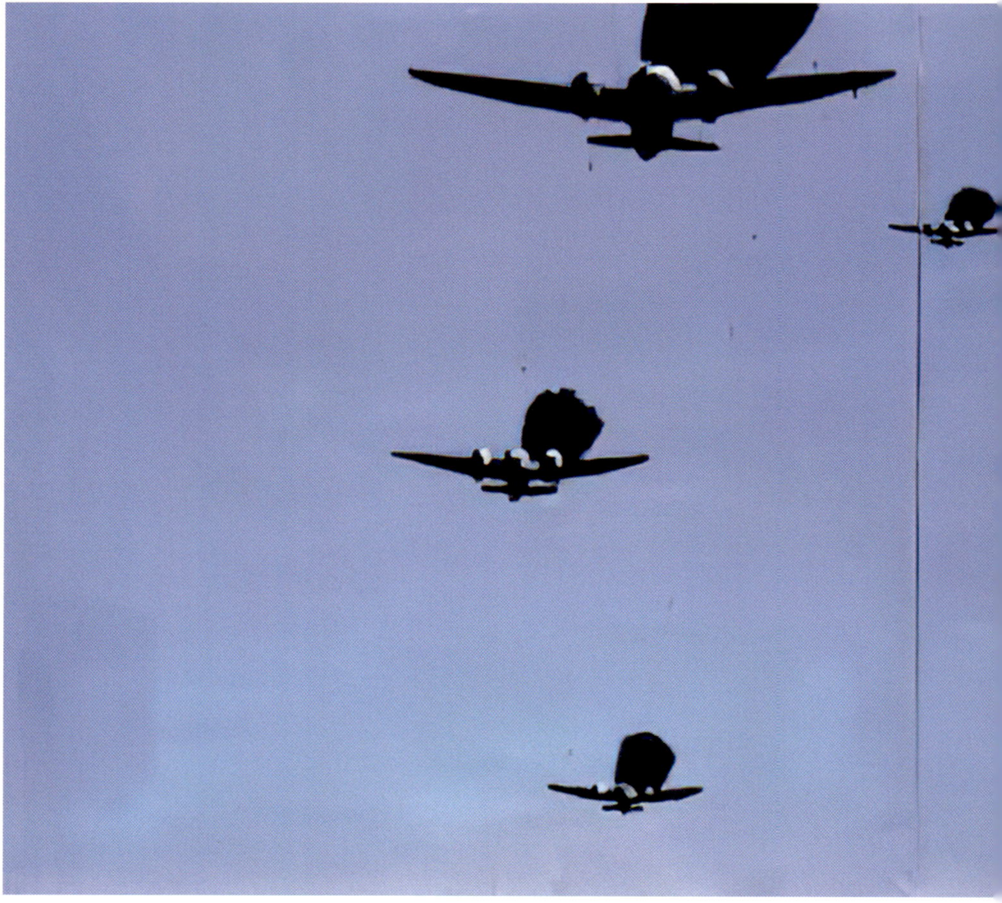

Wilhelm Sasnal
Airplanes 1999 Oil paint on canvas, 1500 × 2997 mm
YAGEO Foundation Collection, Taiwan

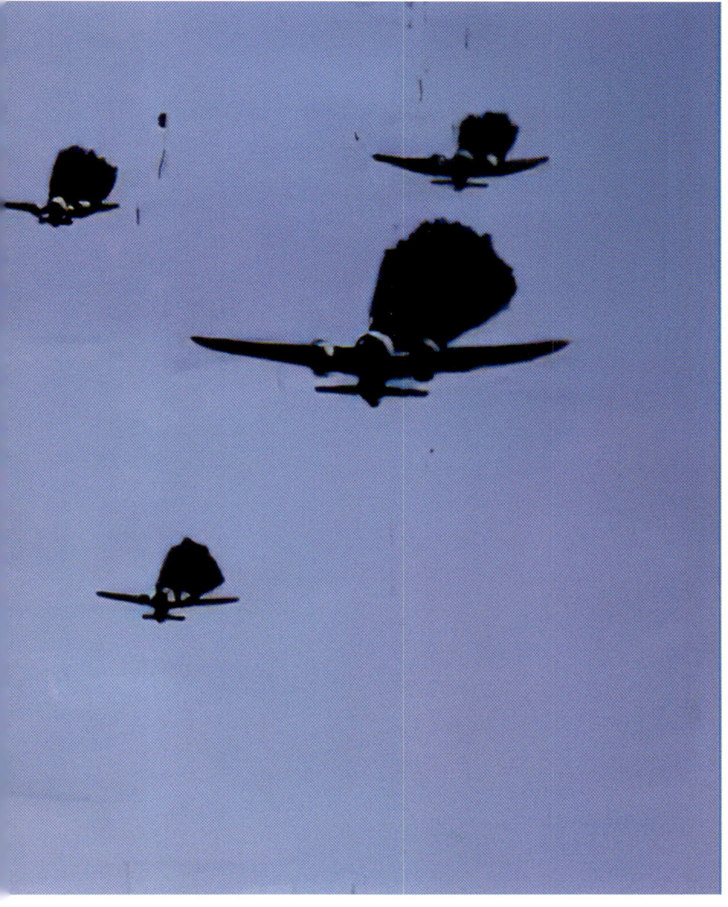

'I think images aren't important because of the numbers that surround us.
But painting has a chance. There is always painting, like there's song.'
                                                              – Wilhelm Sasnal

Convergence

In the 1950s and '60s artists such as Andy Warhol, Robert Rauschenberg, Pauline Boty and Richard Hamilton experimented with the medium of painting. They incorporated screenprinting and photographic sources from popular culture, mass media and advertising into their work. This approach of fusing popular imagery and mechanical processes with high art was embraced by artists around the globe, and came to be known as 'pop' art.

Artists used screenprinting techniques to appropriate, enlarge and multiply photographic material. A mechanical process that subverted concepts of uniqueness and painterly genius, screenprinting mimicked the influx of images and information in an increasingly mediated world. Pop art works refer to other images: Boty, for instance, painted *Portrait of Derek Marlowe with Unknown Ladies* 1962–3 (see page 88) in response to photographic or cinematic footage of Marlowe and Marilyn Monroe.

In this chapter, we see Warhol, Boty and Hamilton capture their world and environment, explore the cult of personality and investigate the sexual politics of popular visual culture. Boty exposes the objectification of women; Warhol and Hamilton the constructed and performative nature of masculinity. By multiplying and enlarging the visual noise of modern life, these works expose the complex relationship between image and self.

Joan Semmel, John Currin, Paulina Olowska, Lisa Brice and Njideka Akunyili Crosby appropriate photographic images from popular culture in order to reclaim and recentre the female body. In doing so, they complicate the relationship between image-making and self-representation. The camera works in Semmel's self-portrait as a lens that depicts the reality of her female body: raw, vulnerable, unidealised. Olowska, Currin and Brice push the photographic towards the fantastical, exploring the relationship between images and truthful representations of womanhood. They subvert depictions of the female body as representations of heterosexual male desire. In a world where images and people are in constant flux, Akunyili Crosby explores how images work to construct a sense of self that is hybrid and culturally complex.

Together, these works ask us to consider how images can offer distorted or authentic representations of womanhood, and how identity is expressed and mediated through culture. Violence, human suffering and conflict have long been subjects of artistic representation, inspiring fascination and discomfort in equal measure. The artists displayed in this section utilise the power of images to portray the violence of the collective human condition. They revel in the creative conflict of painting, allowing sickly palettes, loose brushstrokes, scars or rips to appear in their work.

Horror, in Luc Tuymans', Peter Doig's and Marlene Dumas' works, is rooted in imagination and fiction. Tuymans and Doig draw upon cinematic imagery and the filmic conventions of suspense to create nightmarish dreamscapes that, without depicting violence directly, convey a sense of disquiet. Dumas explores the psychological and visual implications of death in disturbing yet mesmerising portraits inspired by images of dead bodies. Seemingly charged with eroticism, they explore our desire to look and to consume images.

Miriam Cahn and Michael Armitage draw upon documentary footage to depict instances of contemporary political conflict. Vividness and violence collide in Armitage's depiction of Kenya's postcolonial turmoil, while the bodies of migrants drowning at sea in *The Beautiful Blue (Das Schöne Blau)* 2008–17 (see page 92) haunt our consciousness and challenge us to empathise with their loss. Jana Euler explores themes of fear and the unknown through the image of a great white shark (see page 102), occupying and attacking the tradition of painting and its association with masculine gestures.

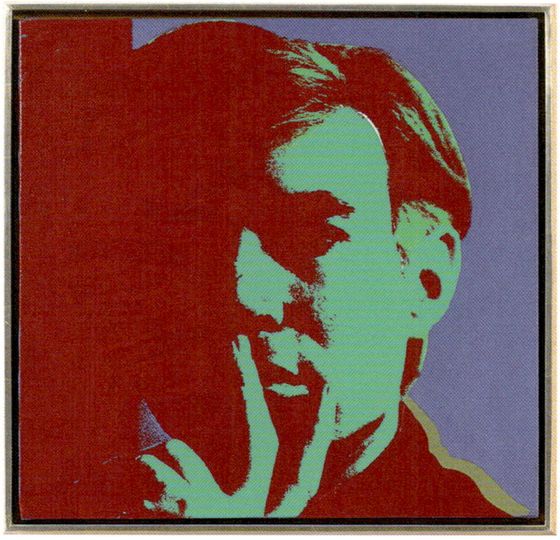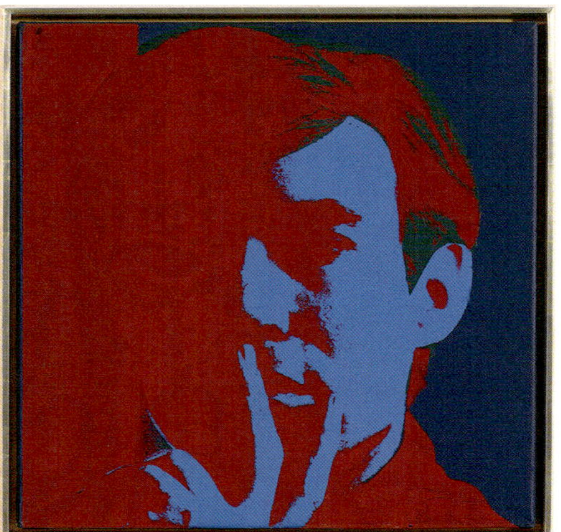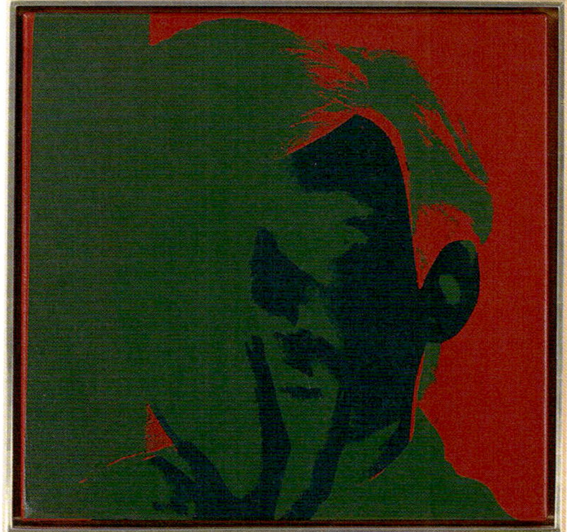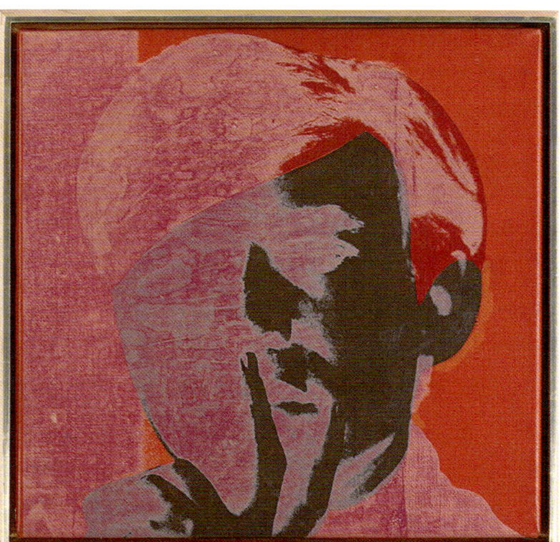

Andy Warhol
Self Portrait 1966–7 Synthetic polymer, acrylic and silkscreen inks on linen, 559 × 559 mm
YAGEO Foundation Collection, Taiwan

Andy Warhol
Self Portrait 1966–7
Brian Dillon

> Okay, B, okay. So now the pimple's covered. But am I covered? I have to look in the mirror for more clues.[1]

In this quartet grid of silkscreen self-portraits, Andy Warhol has coloured himself in. It was a lifetime's work for an artist who felt keenly his physical imperfection – as both torment and opportunity. His bad skin, his thinning hair and fluctuating weight: as a young man, Warhol laboured to conceal or distract from his bodily faults and the strangeness of his presence. A magazine editor, for whom he had worked as a commercial artist, recalled that Warhol was all one pale colour – like a ghost. By the time he completed these self-portraits, which are based on a single, close-cropped photograph, Warhol had learned to make himself more vivid and visible, to take advantage of his blemishes and weaknesses. There exists a washed-out grey version from the same series, in which you can see a lot more detail: the pores on his nose, a plumpness of cheek that he hated, the abrupt hairline that reveals he is wearing a wig.

In these four colour-saturated variants, some information has vanished. Warhol's dreamy gaze is now almost illegible, signalled only by the fingers he has raised thoughtfully to his face – in a gesture with a long history in Western art, at least since the dolorous, reflective figure in Albrecht Dürer's *Melencolia I* 1514. What, if anything, is Warhol hiding by covering himself with colour? And in what sense are these really self-portraits, when he was at other times so much more candid? There are numerous photographic self-portraits in which he flaunts his peculiarities. A Polaroid from 1977, where he appears in profile with his hairpiece awkwardly plastered on. From the same year, wearing a heavy black coat, the lifelong Catholic looks almost priestly. Two years later, in close-up, with eyebrows bleached to match his wig, he seems impossible to fix in age, looking both young and old at once. The visual confusion was surely deliberate.

Warhol used self-portraiture as a disguise, as a means of self-disclosure and as a zone of ambiguity between the two. At times, he is obviously playing a part, as in a sequence of blue silkscreens from 1963–4, based on pictures taken in a photo booth. With his dark glasses, raincoat and askew tie, Warhol mugs for the automatic camera in the guise of a down-at-heel spy or private eye. But some of his assumed roles or personae went deeper than others, meant more to a young gay artist with an uncertain relationship to pop-cultural versions of American masculinity. In one of his earliest silkscreen self-portraits, Warhol faces the viewer head-on; he is wearing a plain T-shirt and looks, in the words of one of his biographers, like 'a perfectly normal young man'.[2] I suspect instead that the image is a knowing homage to Marlon Brando, James Dean and Truman Capote – Warhol masquerading as contemporary images of straight and queer maleness, just as much in drag as he is later, in his self-portraits with full make-up and lavishly feminine wigs.

When he was photographed or painted by others, Warhol again oscillated between a self-protecting persona – the leather jacket, silver hair and sunglasses had solidified by the mid-1960s – and what seems a surprising degree of licence and vulnerability. They were products of the same controlling impulse: passivity and naivety were, after all, aspects of the pose. The most notoriously revealing images are those showing Warhol after he had recovered from his shooting by Valerie Solanas in 1968. In Richard Avedon's 1969 photographs and Alice Neel's 1970 painting, Warhol shows off his scars, making a show of holding himself together. In 1981, Robert Levin photographed him undressing before a skin treatment – in the most striking image, Andy lies shrouded in white, with his eyes closed, like a corpse.

In 1966 or 1967, when the variously hued iterations of the silkscreen *Self Portrait* were made, it seems that Warhol was not yet the artist of an almost gothic interest in his own mortality (only that of others, as the car-crash and electric-chair paintings attest). Repetition, flatness, a realm of colour borrowed from advertising and product packaging: for now, Warhol is all surface, or so he wishes us to believe. In his self-presentation, he embraced this vacancy and flatness, even being photographed with his own self-portraits strapped to his body as if they were old-fashioned advertising sandwich boards. In 1969, *Playboy* magazine ran an article titled 'What's a Warhol?' and asked what might lurk behind his image: '1. bland interior; 2. consummate artist; 3. crown prince of put-ons'.[3] To illustrate the piece, the artist provided what look like parodies of Warhol's earlier self-portraits, this time made with his face against a photocopier and coloured with felt-tip pen.

Of course, the silkscreen *Self Portraits* are also exercises and experiments in colour, with the outlines and textures of Warhol's face insisting or retreating to different degrees, depending on the combination of colours and the finish produced by the silkscreen process, which was rarely as seamless or inhuman as Warhol or his interpreters claimed. The deficiencies that Warhol sometimes hid and sometimes flaunted: they are here transmuted into accidents of colour and texture. In other paintings and photographs, Warhol performed his own frailty and admitted the falsities of his image. In a series of paintings from 1978, his face appears alongside a plainly artificial human skull. In the decade following, shortly before his death in 1987, he made several works titled *Self-Portrait in Fright Wig*: no pretence any more to 'normality'. In the 1960s self-portraits, he gives himself away only on the surface of the painting, and in its repetitions.

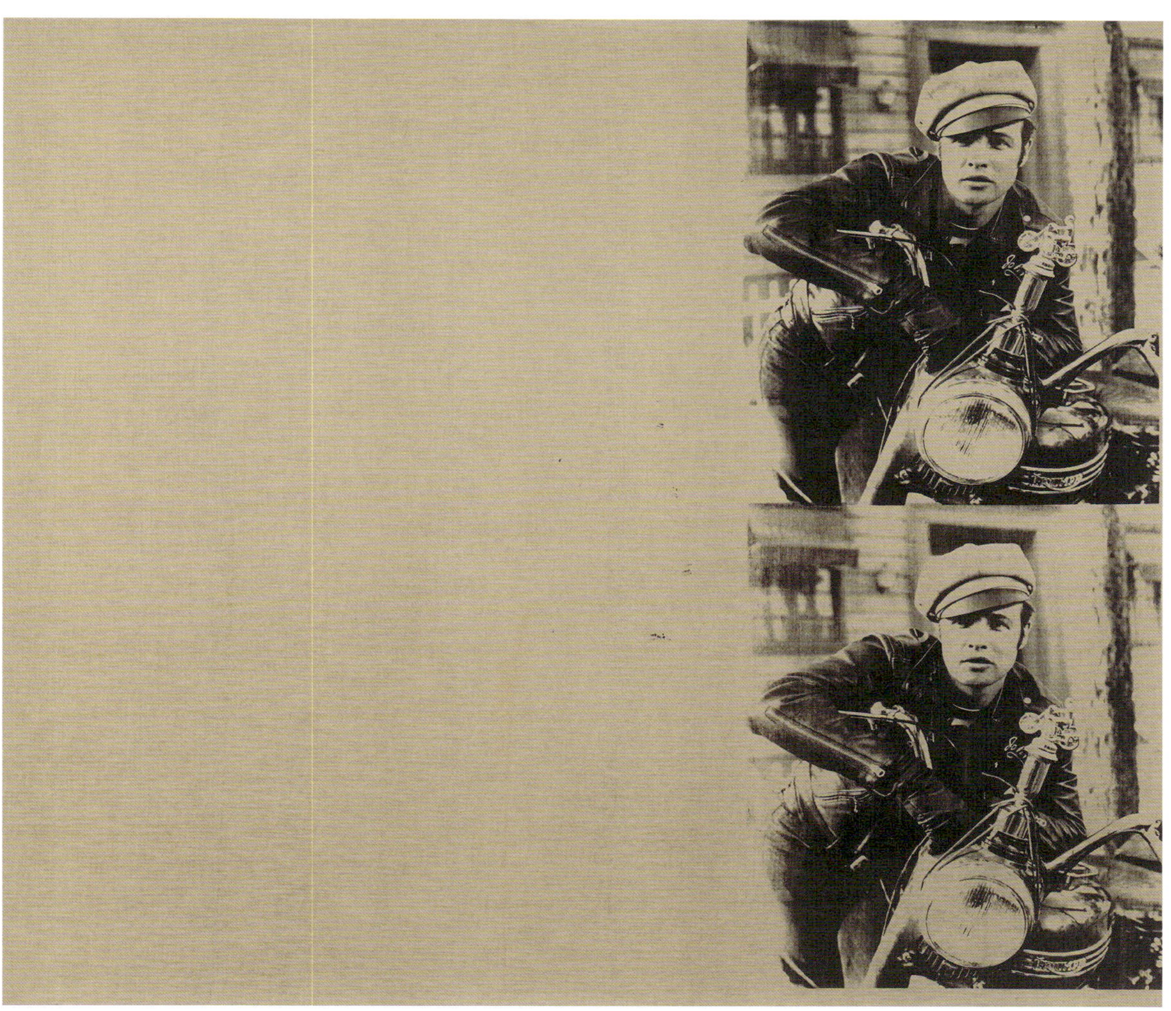

Andy Warhol
Double Marlon 1966 Silkscreen on linen, 2430 × 2134 mm
YAGEO Foundation Collection, Taiwan

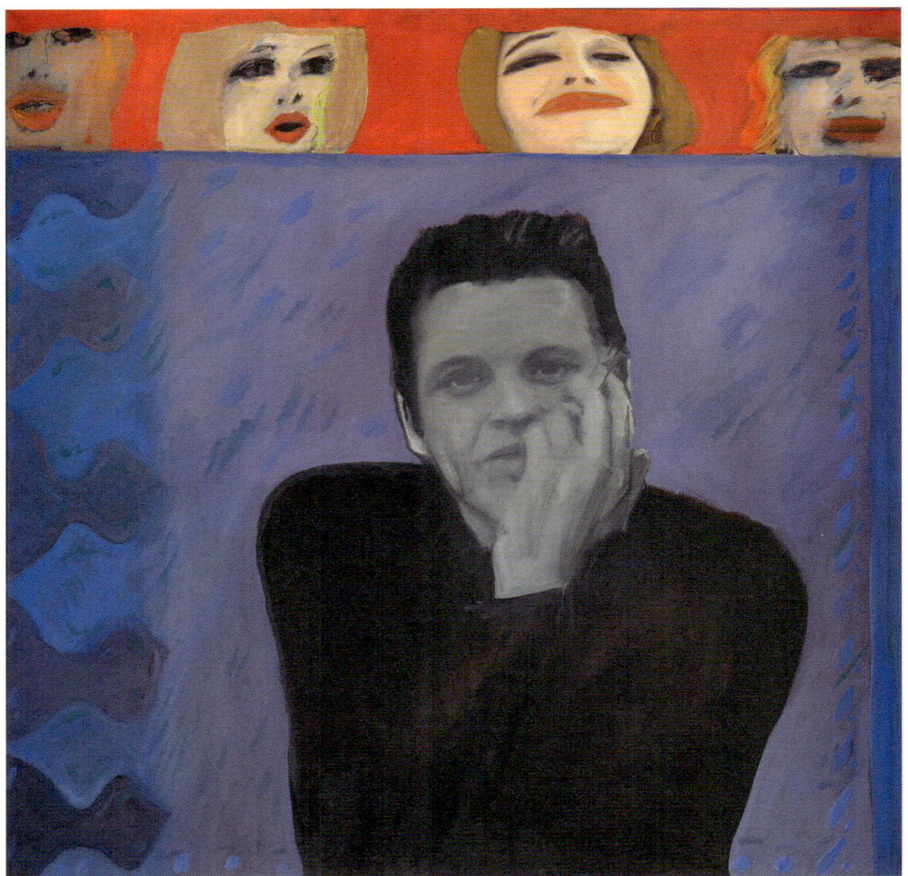

Pauline Boty
Portrait of Derek Marlowe with Unknown Ladies 1962–3 Oil paint on canvas, 1222 × 1224 mm

Tate, purchased with funds provided by the Denise Coates Foundation on the occasion of the 2018 centenary of women gaining the right to vote in Britain 2018

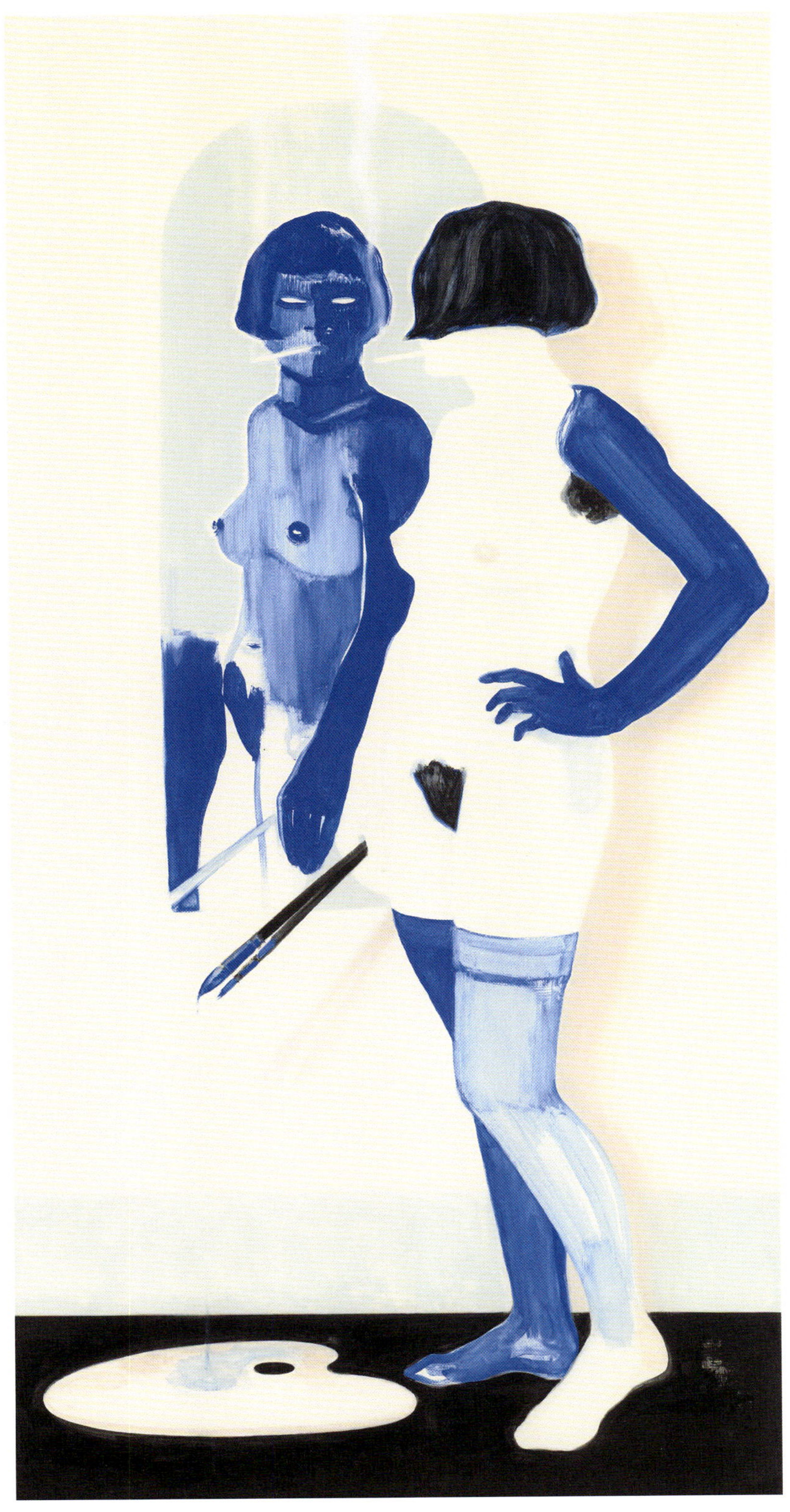

Lisa Brice
Untitled 2019 Gouache and tempera on canvas, 2000 × 950 mm
Tate, presented by Harry and Lana David 2020

'I am drawn to the ambiguity that people and places can hold. Sometimes the compositions of my paintings feel like cinematic outtakes: the moments between directed actions, when the figures are "on their own time," self-involved, performing only for themselves or one another.'

– Lisa Brice

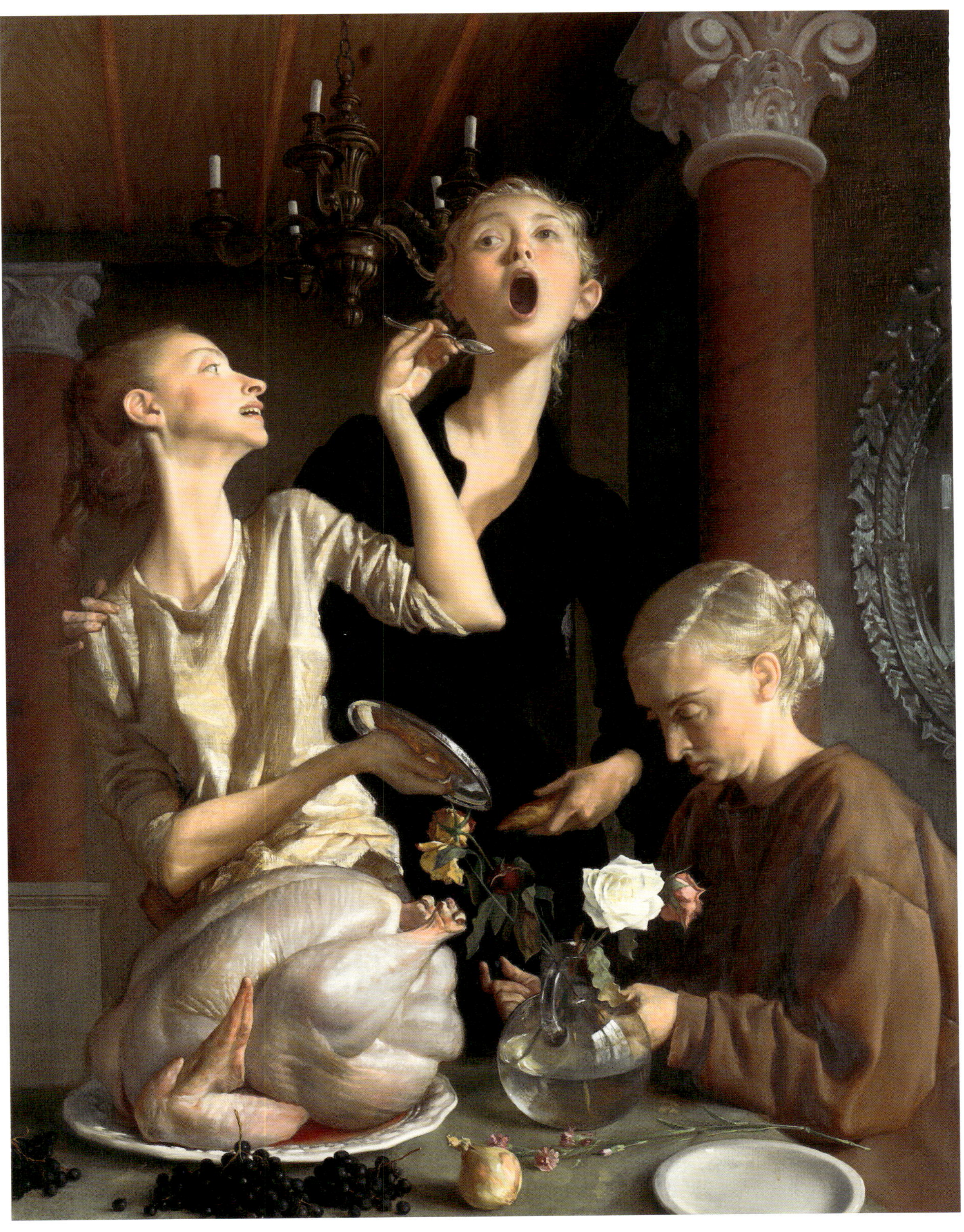

John Currin
Thanksgiving 2003 Oil paint on canvas, 1729 × 1323 mm
Tate, purchased with funds provided by the Acquisitions Fund for African Art supported by Guaranty Trust Bank Plc 2014

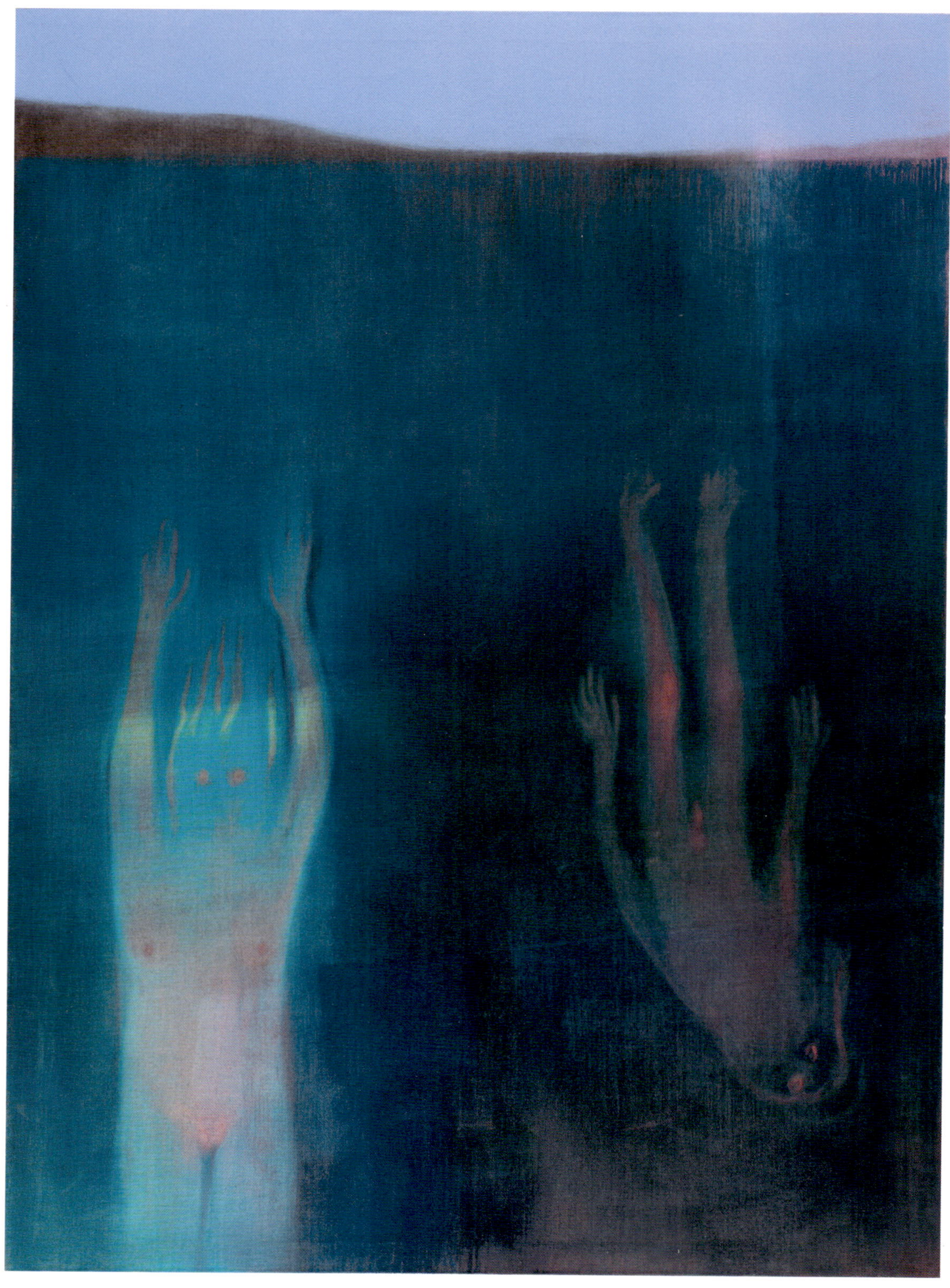

Miriam Cahn
The Beautiful Blue (Das Schöne Blau) 2008–17 Oil paint on canvas, 2504 × 1803 mm
Tate, purchased with funds provided by The Joe and Marie Donnelly Acquisition Fund 2020

Miriam Cahn
The Beautiful Blue (Das Schöne Blau) 2008–17
Ismail Einashe

The Swiss artist Miriam Cahn's startling painting *The Beautiful Blue* depicts a harrowing scene of two figures – one female, the other male – sinking into a dark sea beneath a bright, cloudless sky. The woman falls with her arms outstretched as if she had jumped feet-first into the water, while the man descends head first. The blue surrounding them appears at once tranquil and foreboding. Their eyes are reduced to haunting, lifeless dots, and their bodies share trails of red that stretch from their limbs to their cores. A shaft of light across the woman's forehead is hopeful but fleeting, dull by the time it reaches the man's knees as the bodies fall to their fate. Inspired by the movement of refugees and migrants across the Mediterranean, this ghostly work brings to the fore the treacherous journeys and deaths of those who risk all in search of safety and hope.

In 2015, Europe witnessed a rapid increase in migrants and refugees, with 1.3 million people seeking asylum. This marked the most significant number of arrivals in a single year since the Second World War, leading to what became known as the 'migrant crisis'.[1] Most of these individuals came from Syria, Afghanistan, Iraq and Eritrea and were driven by various factors, including conflict, economic hardship and climate change.[2] Since the beginning of the 'crisis' and beyond, hundreds of thousands of migrants and refugees have crossed the Mediterranean to Europe, travelling along exceptionally dangerous migratory routes that claim thousands of lives every year.

Cahn is no stranger to spotlighting contentious subjects. Often described as an 'activist artist', she has traversed boundaries in her decades-long practice, capturing subjects from violence against women to conflict in Iraq and the representations of refugees in the Balkans.[3] With palpable anger, her work questions the prevailing norms that disregard humans in need, and pushes us, the viewers, to rethink our perceptions. In *The Beautiful Blue*, Cahn reminds us not only about the plight of those forced to embark on perilous journeys but also challenges us to make sense of the narratives that have shaped our collective perceptions of migrants. More than a piece of art, the work is a mirror held up to society, reflecting its ugly blemishes.

The trouble is that our view of migrants is woven through a highly problematic media lens,[4] which consistently frames migrants as either victims or intruders, reducing their stories and experiences to mere debate points and side-lining their humanity.[5] We skim through images of small boats, barbed wire and faceless masses accompanied by reportage pre-laden with alarmist narratives (are they here to steal our jobs? Do they pose a threat to our way of life?)

In September 2023, a record number of people crossed the Mediterranean and arrived on the Italian island of Lampedusa to seek refuge in Europe. Conservative politicians and newspapers used inflammatory, degrading terms (like 'surge', 'overwhelmed', 'flooded', 'illegal' and 'invasion') to condemn their arrival, portraying it as a dangerous occupation rather than a humanitarian emergency.[6] Framed another way, we might recognise that these migrants and refugees had arrived on a continent of over 700 million people with an economy of $24 trillion rooted in colonial plunder, mass capitalist extraction and climate damage. Yet, we rarely hear this expressed in media coverage.

Cahn's depiction of two figures drowning in the Mediterranean points to the callous indifference with which Europe has treated the needless deaths of migrants in the expanse of water the Romans christened *mare nostrum* (in Latin, 'our sea'). (In his concluding comments during a recent conference held in the port city of Marseille, Pope Francis warned that the Mediterranean is becoming 'the *mare mortuum*, the graveyard of dignity')[7] Cahn's work might make us think of the Italian academic Alessandra Di Maio's use of the term the 'Black Mediterranean' to spotlight how this sea is a racialised border guarded with the tools of oppression.

Cahn has consistently harnessed her art to capture uncomfortable truths about society. Yet what sets her work apart is a profoundly empathic approach towards her subjects. Though her work confronts us with harrowing visuals, there's a clear intent to disarm the prevailing negative lens and restore a sense of shared humanity. The artist has described how she draws from her Jewish roots to empathise with migrants from outside Europe (she once said it was her 'duty' to use her position to spotlight the pain of others).[8] Other thoughtful artistic reflections on the 2015 mass migration include *2016* by Maggi Hambling, in which an upturned boat disappears beneath rippling waves as light flickers off the choppy blue waters. Rather than painting from a single photograph, Hambling based the work on photos and news reports she came across, underscoring how the images of the 'crisis' have fundamentally shaped our view of migrants.[9] Similarly, Cahn offers a dynamic window into the individual migration experience.

In *The Beautiful Blue*, Cahn creates a space for us to explore the power of art as a means to express profound truths. The work beckons us to look beyond the surface, to see the humanity in every migrant and to recognise the profound acts of survival and imagination that drive their journeys. It reminds us that the migrant experience is not only shaped by political, media or economic narratives but is, at its heart, a deeply personal, human experience. By viewing the migration experience in this way, through the lens of contemporary art, we free it from being measured solely by its political or economic dimensions and, in doing so, its shape emerges fuller, more profound, humane and truthful.[10]

Although *The Beautiful Blue* depicts an unspeakable tragic scene, it also speaks to the migrants' journey of setting out in hope. In Somali, the term *buufis* relates to this idea. Meaning 'to blow' or 'inflate', it encapsulates a sense of yearning to find a new home abroad. The word also evokes the spiritual dimensions of migration in a culture marked by decades of displacement. This could include Somali refugees living in Dadaab, Kenya's largest refugee camp, or those who arrived in Britain in the 1990s, like my own family.

Looking at Cahn's painting, it's hard not to feel a surge of emotion, perhaps a sense of empathy. It becomes clear that acts of migration aren't just about survival but are profound displays of hope, courage and imagination. And as art shows us, imagination knows no borders – it can take us anywhere we dare to dream.

'Photographs are haptic objects, meaning that they're not just taken as something we're supposed to see, but that photographs are made or have historically been made to be touched, to be handed from one person to the next.'

– Tina Campt

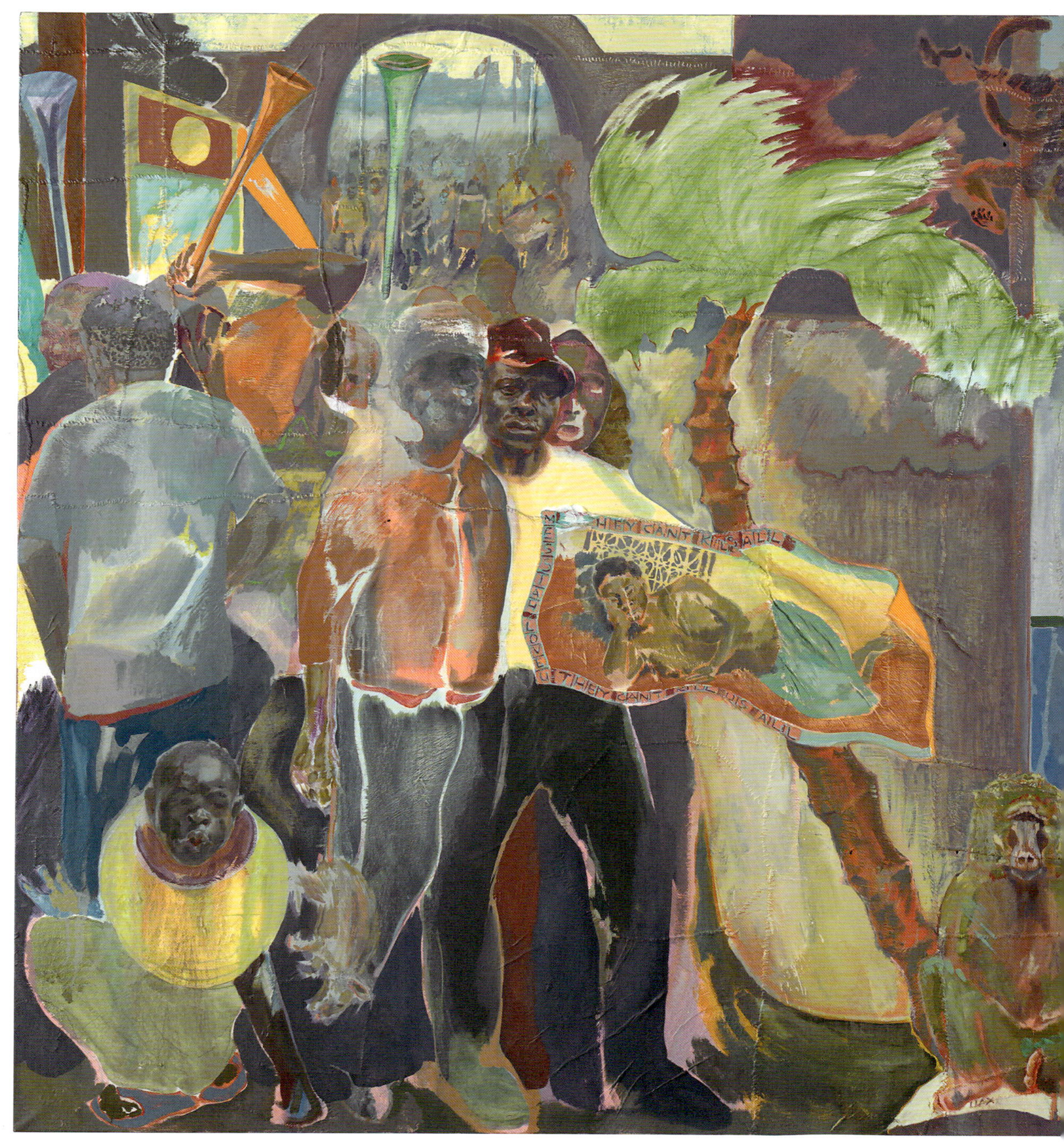

Michael Armitage
The Promised Land 2019 Oil paint, acrylic paint, graphite and chalk pastel on bark cloth, 2210 × 4210 mm
Tate, purchased with funds provided by Harry and Lana David 2022

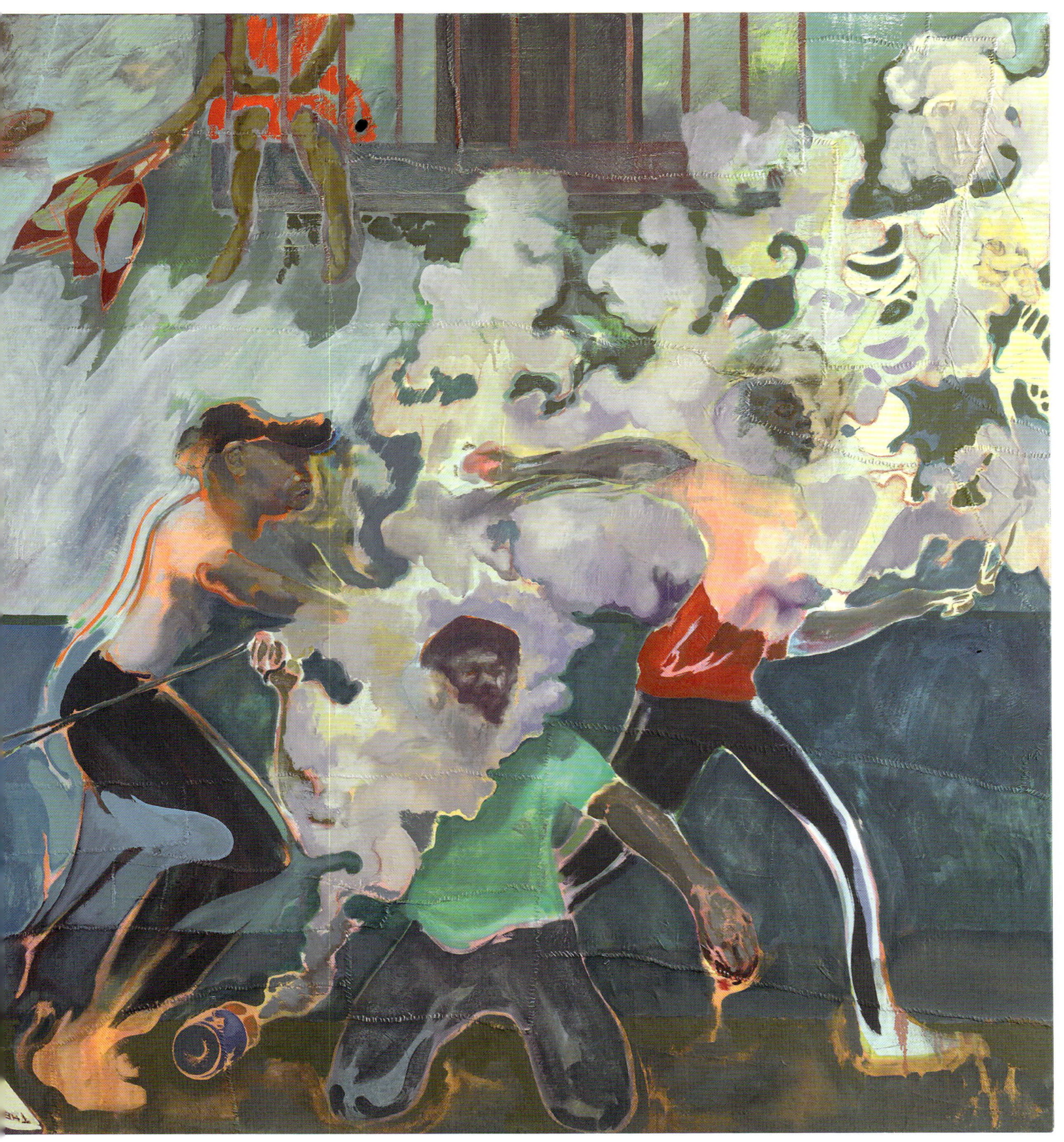

'When I started to paint on the [*lubugo* bark] cloth, the surface, heavily textured with divots, holes, stitching and the grain of the bark, would disrupt the way that the paint came off the brush – it was almost anti-painting.'

– Michael Armitage

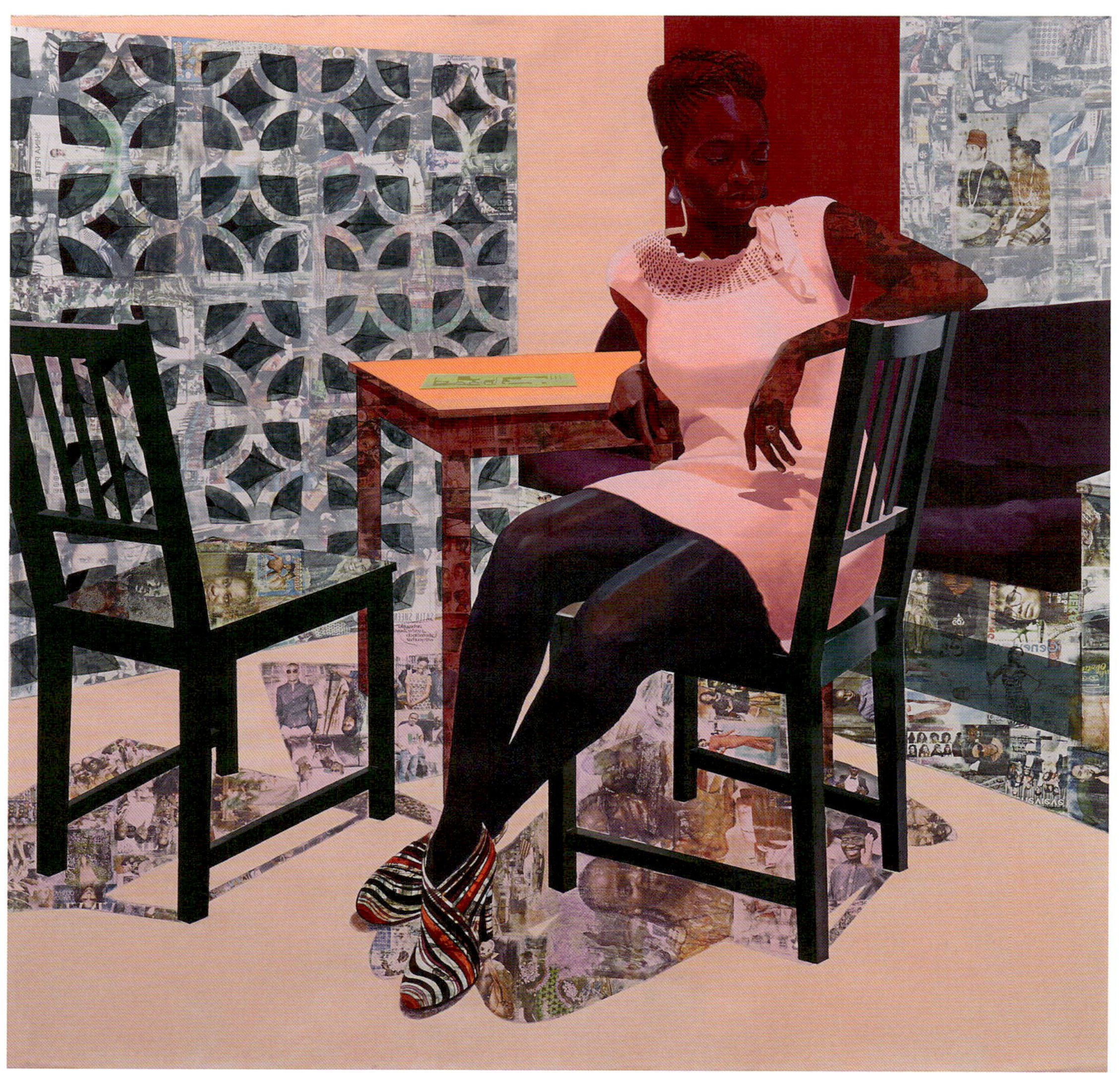

Njideka Akunyili Crosby
Predecessors 2013 Two works on paper, charcoal, acrylic paint, graphite and transfer print, each 2120 × 2123 mm
Tate, purchased with funds provided by the Acquisitions Fund for African Art supported by Guaranty Trust Bank Plc 2014

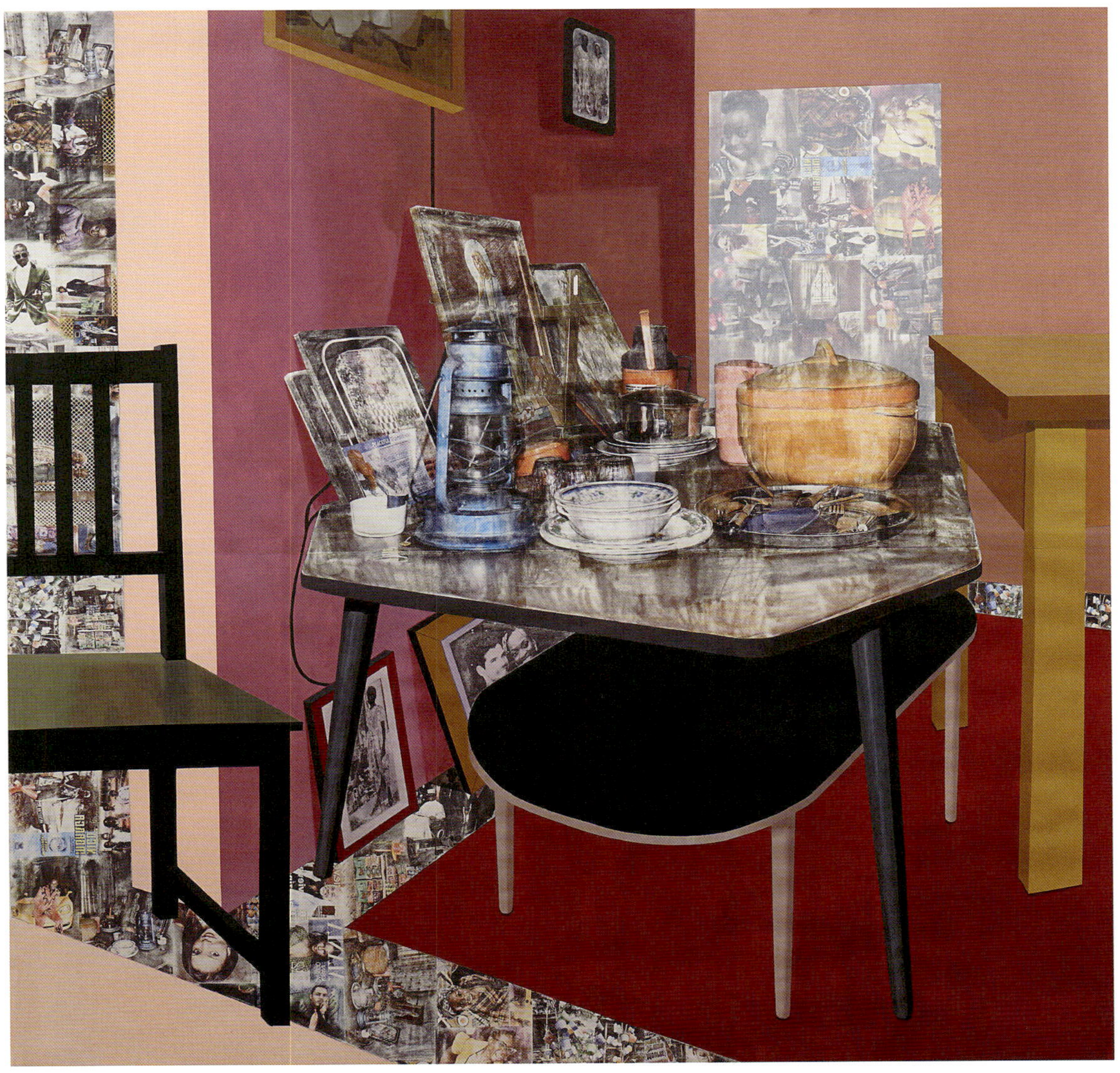

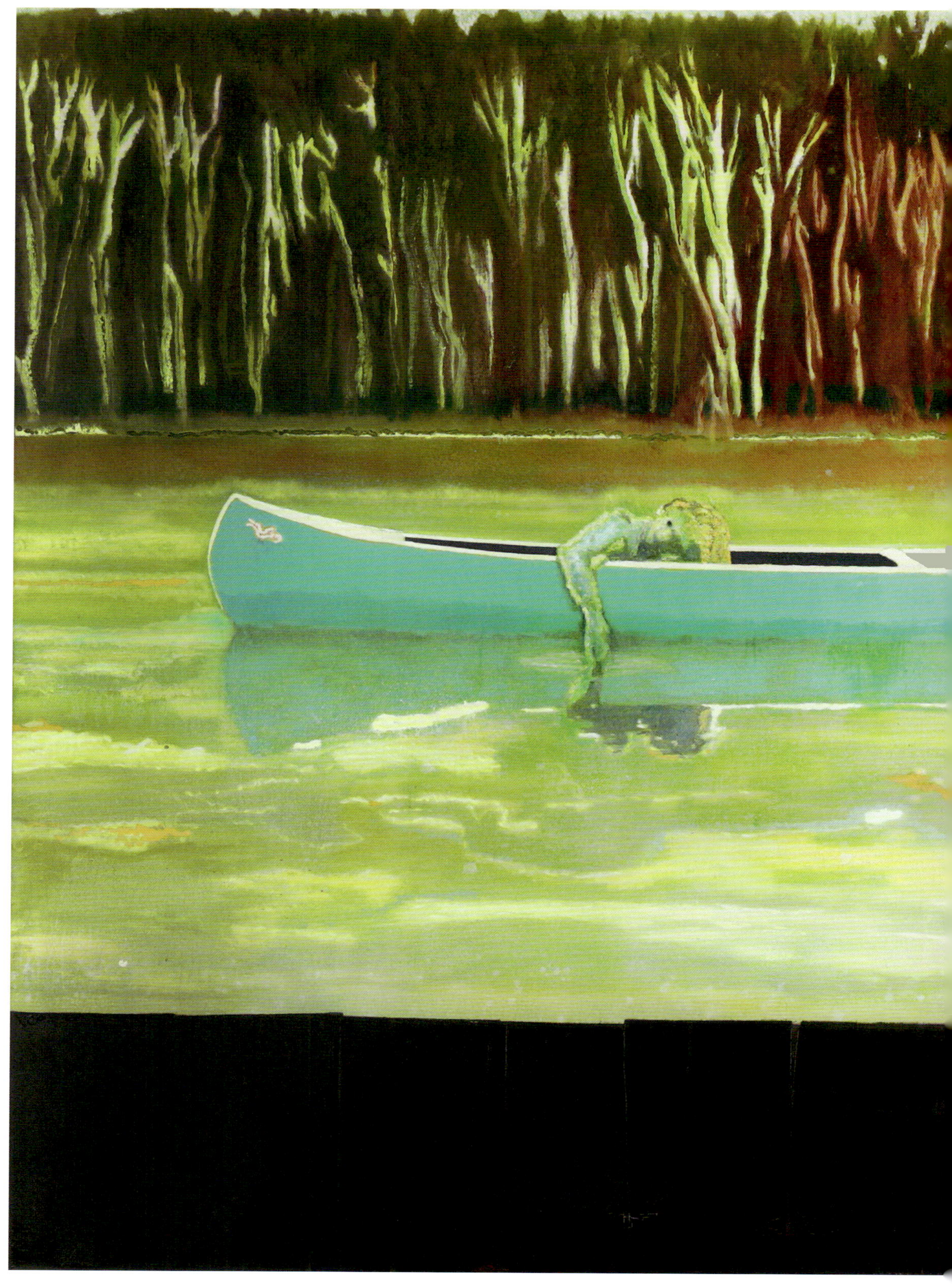

Peter Doig
Canoe Lake 1997–8, Oil paint on canvas, 2000 × 3000 mm
YAGEO Foundation Collection, Taiwan

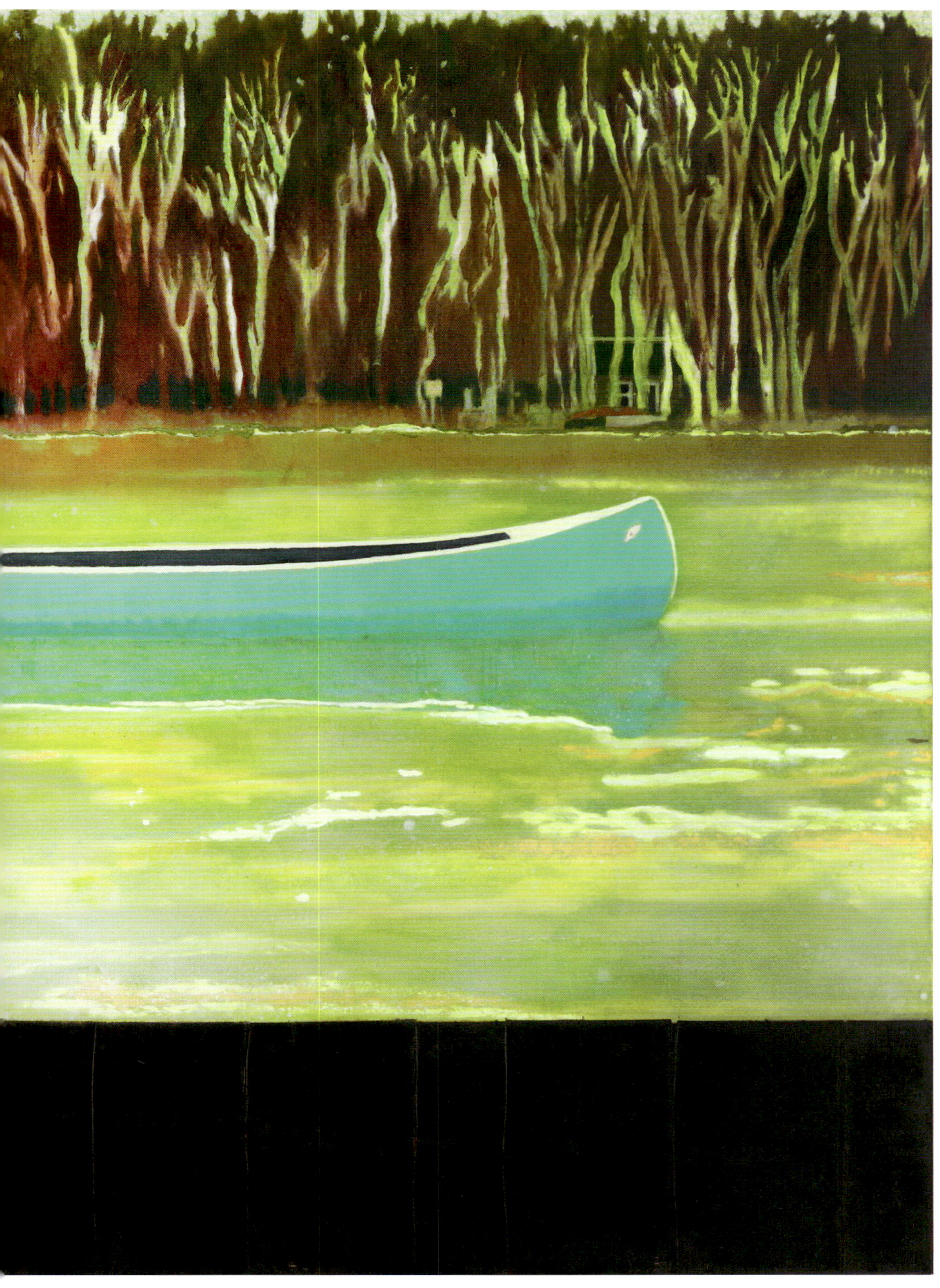

'I use the photo like a map, but it is not a tracing, just a way of giving me a foot into a kind of reality that I want.'

– Peter Doig

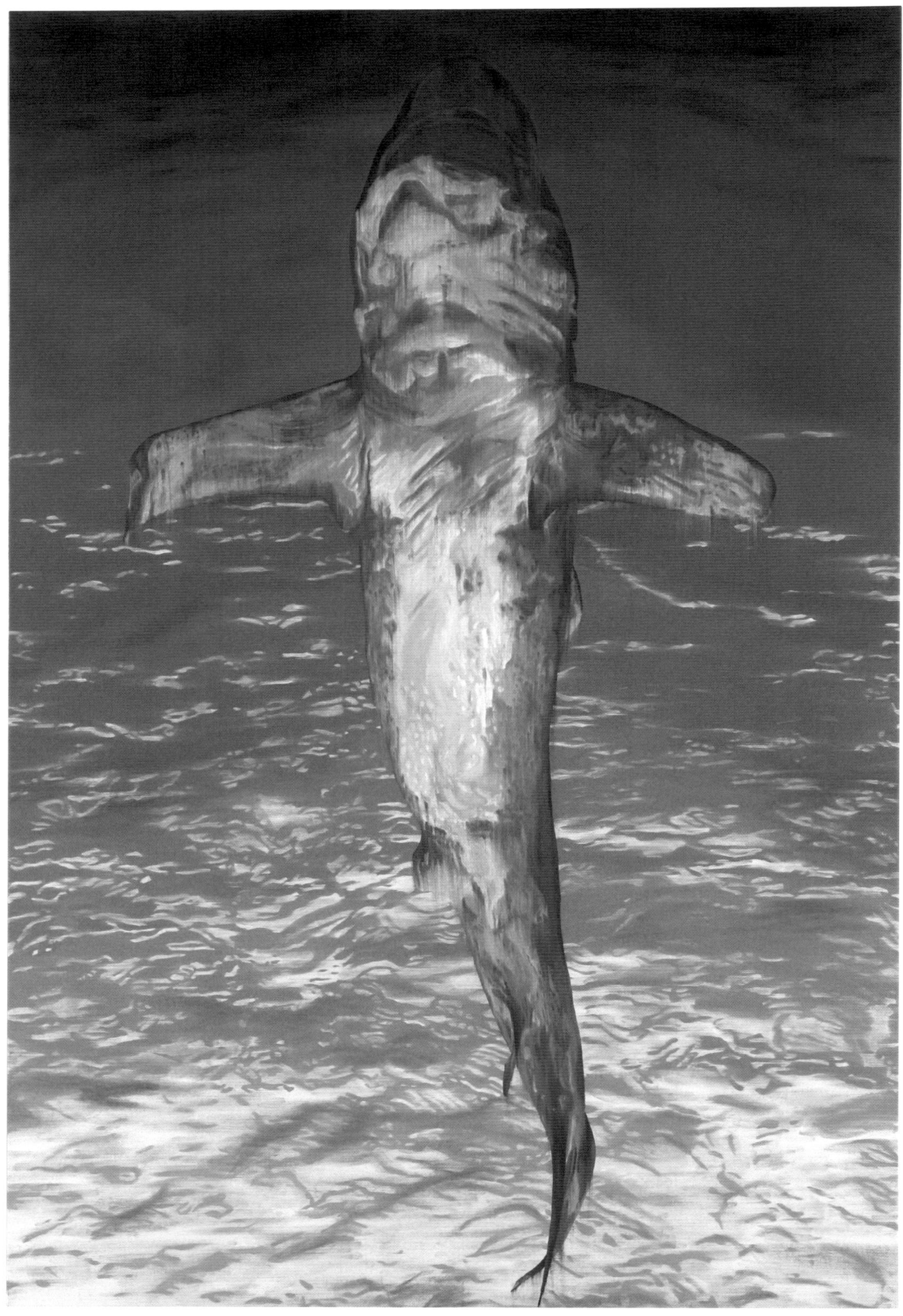

Jana Euler
gwf 9, Richter/Baselitz 2019 Oil paint on canvas, 3002 × 2002 mm

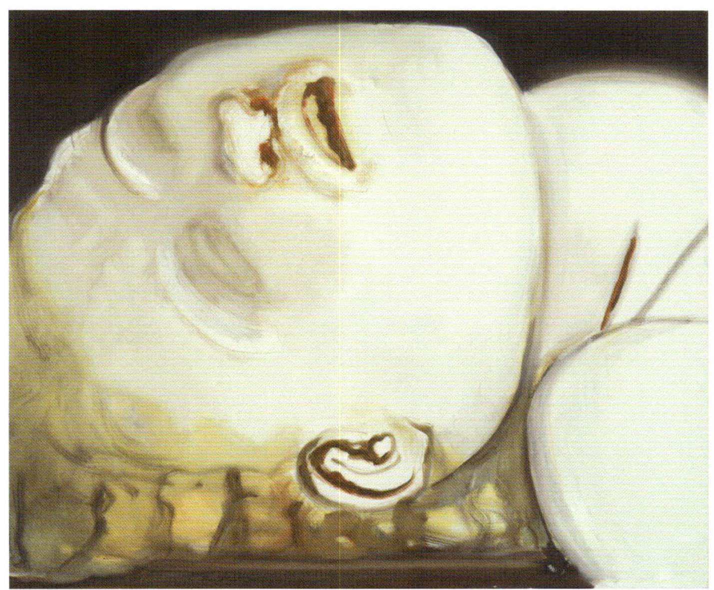

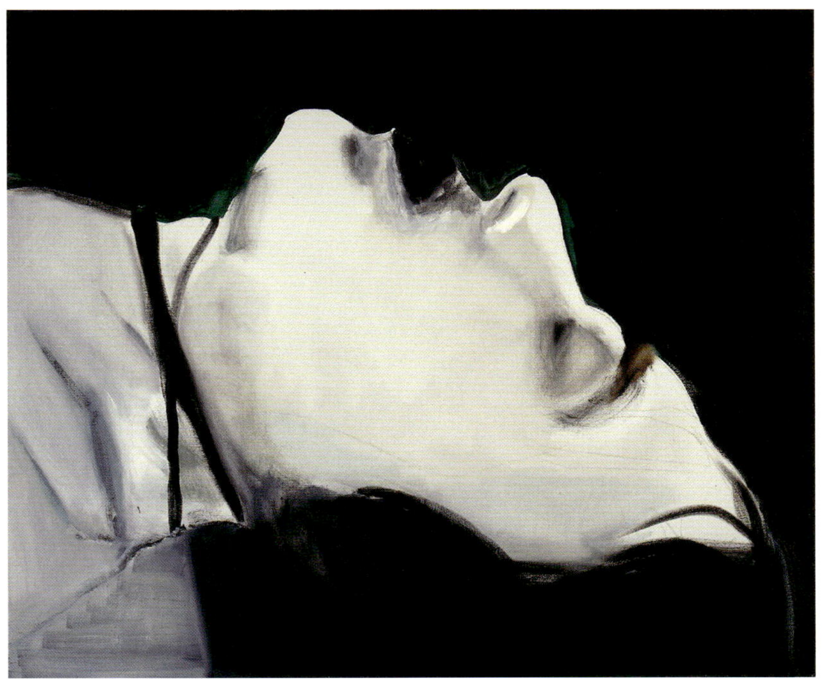

Marlene Dumas
Lucy 2004 Oil paint on canvas, 1103 × 1303 × 24 mm
Stern 2004 Oil paint on canvas, 1101 × 1302 × 24 mm
Tate, purchased with assistance from Foundation Dutch Artworks and Bank Giro Loterij 2007

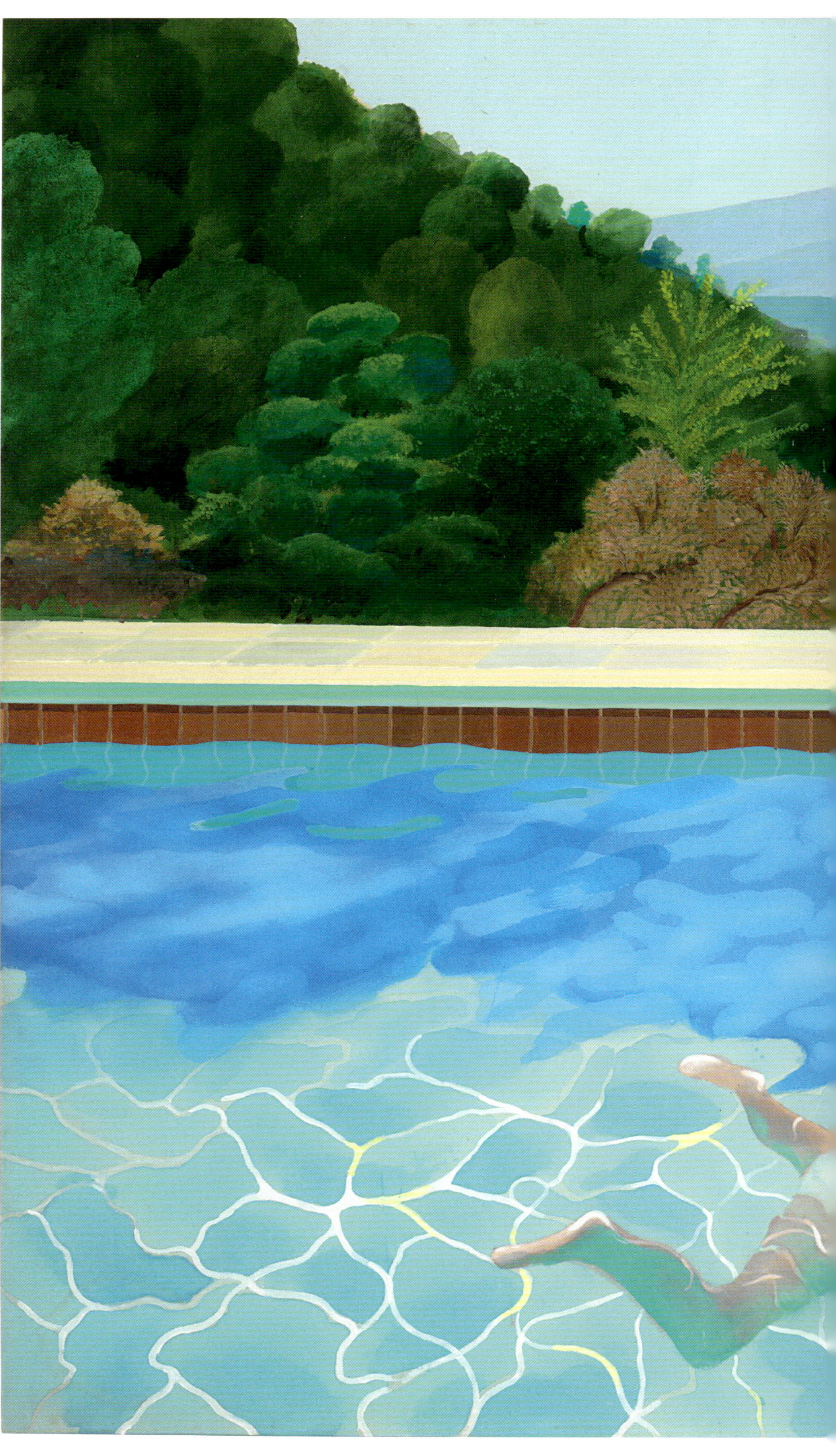

David Hockney
Portrait of an Artist (Pool with Two Figures) 1972 Acrylic paint on canvas, 2135 × 3050 mm
YAGEO Foundation Collection, Taiwan

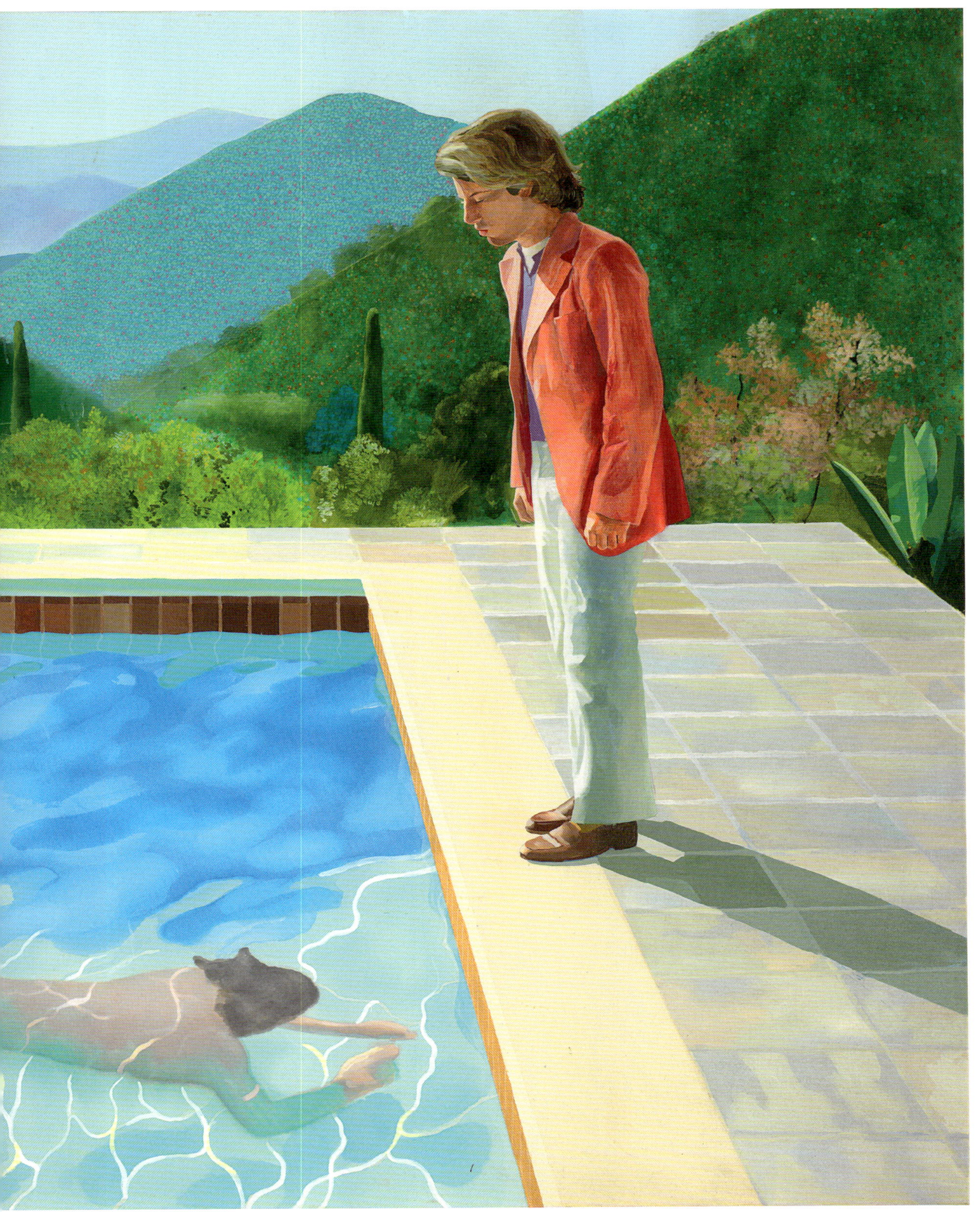

David Hockney
Portrait of an Artist (Pool with Two Figures) 1972
Martin Gayford

The origin of David Hockney's *Portrait of an Artist (Pool with Two Figures)* was an accident. It was the kind of event you might associate with an artist imbued with surrealist ideas about chance – such as Francis Bacon – rather than Hockney. The fortuitous juxtaposition of two otherwise unrelated photographs gave rise to the idea for a painting.

By Hockney's account, one day he glanced down at the floor of his studio and saw two snapshots side by side. 'One', he remembered, 'was of a figure swimming underwater and therefore quite distorted'.[1] This photo had been taken in Hollywood in 1966 when Hockney was working on his celebrated swimming pool paintings. The other was 'of a boy gazing at something on the ground'.

Ostensibly, the second had nothing to do with the first. But according to Hockney, 'because of the way the photographs were lying, it looked as though [the boy] was gazing at the distorted figure'. This instantly fired his imagination. 'I began the painting immediately'.[2]

This spontaneous process of creation suggests that the impetus behind the painting was formal, as indeed was often the case with Hockney's investigations of water and reflection. As he explained many years later, 'It seems to me an interesting thing to do, to draw transparency, because – visually – it's about something not being there, almost. The swimming pool paintings I did were about transparency: how would you paint water? A nice problem, it seemed to me'.[3]

The random placement of the two snapshots must have suggested a novel twist on a frequent Hockney theme of the period: two figures related in one composition. In the late 1960s and early 1970s, Hockney painted a number of two-figure compositions, including several double portraits. In all of these works, the two figures were presented in sharp contrast – often with one full face, one in profile, like a fifteenth-century Italian painting. (In his 1969 portrait of curator Henry Geldzahler and his then-partner, the painter Christopher Scott, Hockney compared the perspective contraction around Geldzahler to a Piero della Francesca and his portrayal of Scott to an early-Renaissance depiction of an angel). The photographs on Hockney's studio floor prompted a further possibility: two figures in completely dissimilar environments – one immersed in water, one not.

So far, the origins of *Portrait of an Artist* seem austerely formal. But the haunting atmosphere of the picture also suggests psychological depths. Roberta Smith of the *New York Times* described it as 'a complex, emotion[al] drama inspired by a personal relationship', arguing that it was a product of the break-up of Hockney's love affair with Peter Schlesinger.[4]

Chronology suggests this might be so. Hockney and Schlesinger had a dramatic row while on holiday during the late summer of 1971, which effectively ended their relationship. Hockney recalled that afterwards, he was 'so unhappy there was nothing to do but work'.[5] That September, he began numerous new paintings, including *Portrait of an Artist*. The moment he saw the two photos on the studio floor must have occurred within weeks of this romantic trauma.

On the other hand, Schlesinger is sceptical of this interpretation. 'I can't speak to its emotional element because I don't think it is emotional', he told the *Observer*. Schlesinger believes the work is concerned with the problems of painting a figure underwater. He added, 'I don't even think it's a portrait of me, really'.[6]

It is, as Hockney has reflected, extremely difficult to know what is going on in a picture. But in this one, there certainly seems to be a sense of separation, a poignant distance between the two figures in contrasting elements. Perhaps this gives the work a sense of longing.

Its genesis was difficult. Hockney struggled with the first version of the painting for months. But, according to him, the problems it presented were technical. What he was trying to do was meld two photographs – taken from different angles, at separated times and places – into one coherent space.

This was part of a larger conundrum. Around 1970, Hockney was trying to combine a naturalistic, photo-based vision with the spatial clarity he admired in the paintings of Piero della Francesca. Eventually, the tension between these aims led him to stylistic crisis. Within a few years, he was to begin his long, love-hate investigation of the shortcomings of photography. Looking back, he felt, 'There was something wrong with what I was doing – I've called it "obsessive naturalism" – but then I didn't know what it was'.[7] In the early 1980s, he began making collages of Polaroid snaps, piecing together dozens to make one image. Subsequently, he made quasi-cubist mosaics with hundreds of photographic prints. More recently, Hockney has used digital photography and made films with multiple, separately angled cameras. The aim of all this activity is to create a picture that is closer to the way we actually see, which is not through one lens with a fixed point of view but through two eyes in constant motion. Our minds piece together innumerable fleeting glimpses received via our retinas, or, as Hockney puts it, 'we see in bits, and link one bit with another bit and another bit'.[8]

But in 1972, this was all in the future. After four months spent struggling to make a coherent image from his two snapshots, it suddenly dawned on Hockney what was wrong with *Portrait of an Artist*: 'it was the angle of the pool which was causing me all the problems'.[9] This can be seen in photographs of the first version of the work, which Hockney destroyed. In this earlier version, there was a higher vantage point, which was far less effective. With only two and a half weeks before an important exhibition, Hockney embarked on a whirlwind repainting on a fresh canvas – and triumphantly succeeded.

The studies for the second version of *Portrait of an Artist* were largely from two photo shoots: one poolside shoot at a villa in the South of France, and the other, a series of Schlesinger posing in Kensington Gardens. But it feels as if there was a third, more lucidly structured source. This, one guesses, could have been a memory of Piero's *Legend of the True Cross* frescoes in Arezzo, one of which features the figure of a workman gazing down into a cavity in the ground with rolling, distant hills behind. The Hockney work seems to echo this.

So, who was the 'artist' of the title? Hockney's friend Geldzahler thought it was Schlesinger, as the picture marked the beginning of the latter's life as an artist. But titles, like pictures, can contain more than one meaning. Perhaps the figure peering into the elusive waters of that pool also stands for Hockney himself.

'A photograph is a fraction of a second, frozen. So, the moment you've looked at it for even four seconds, you're looking at it far more than the camera did.'

– David Hockney

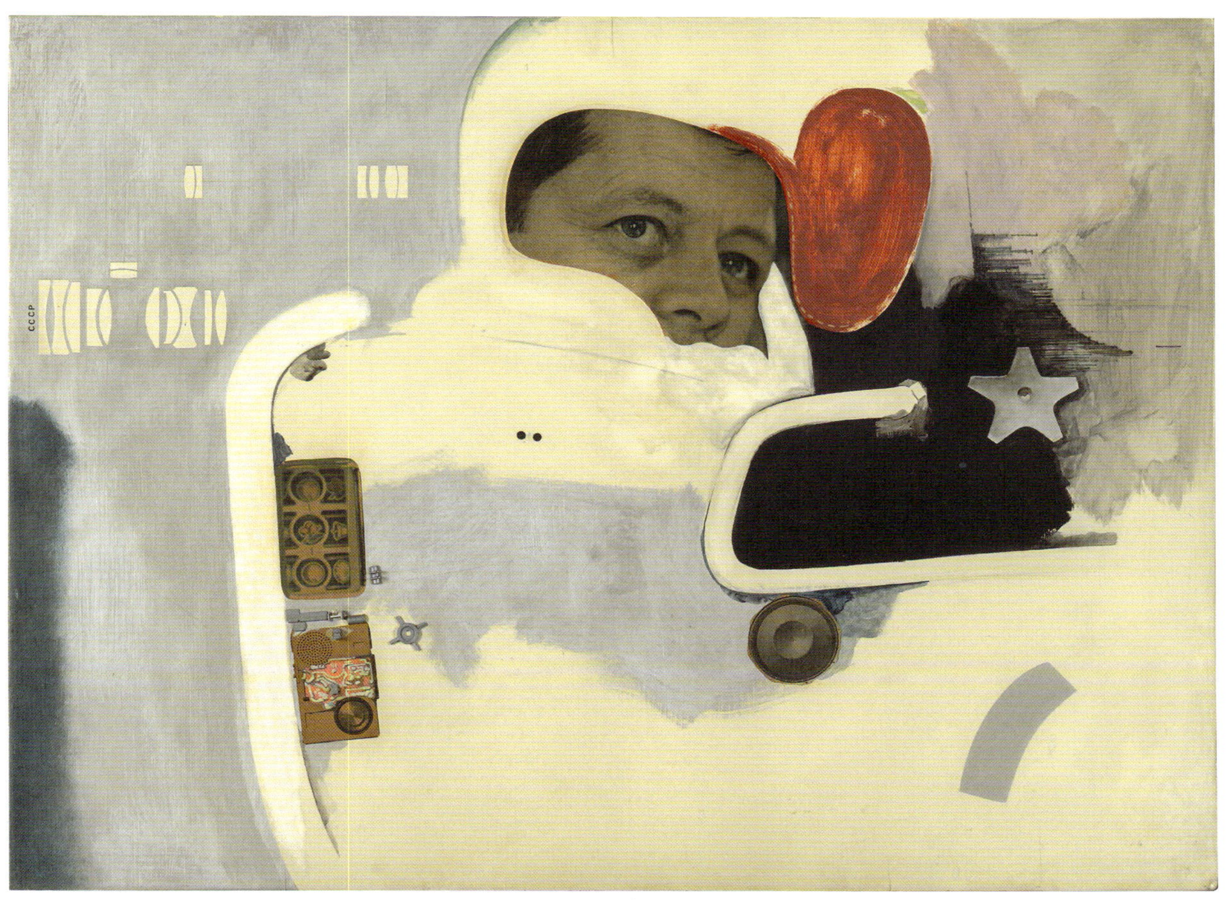

Richard Hamilton
Towards a definitive statement on the coming trends in menswear and accessories (a) / Together let us explore the stars 1962 Oil paint, cellulose paint and printed paper on wood, 610 × 813 mm
Tate, purchased 1964

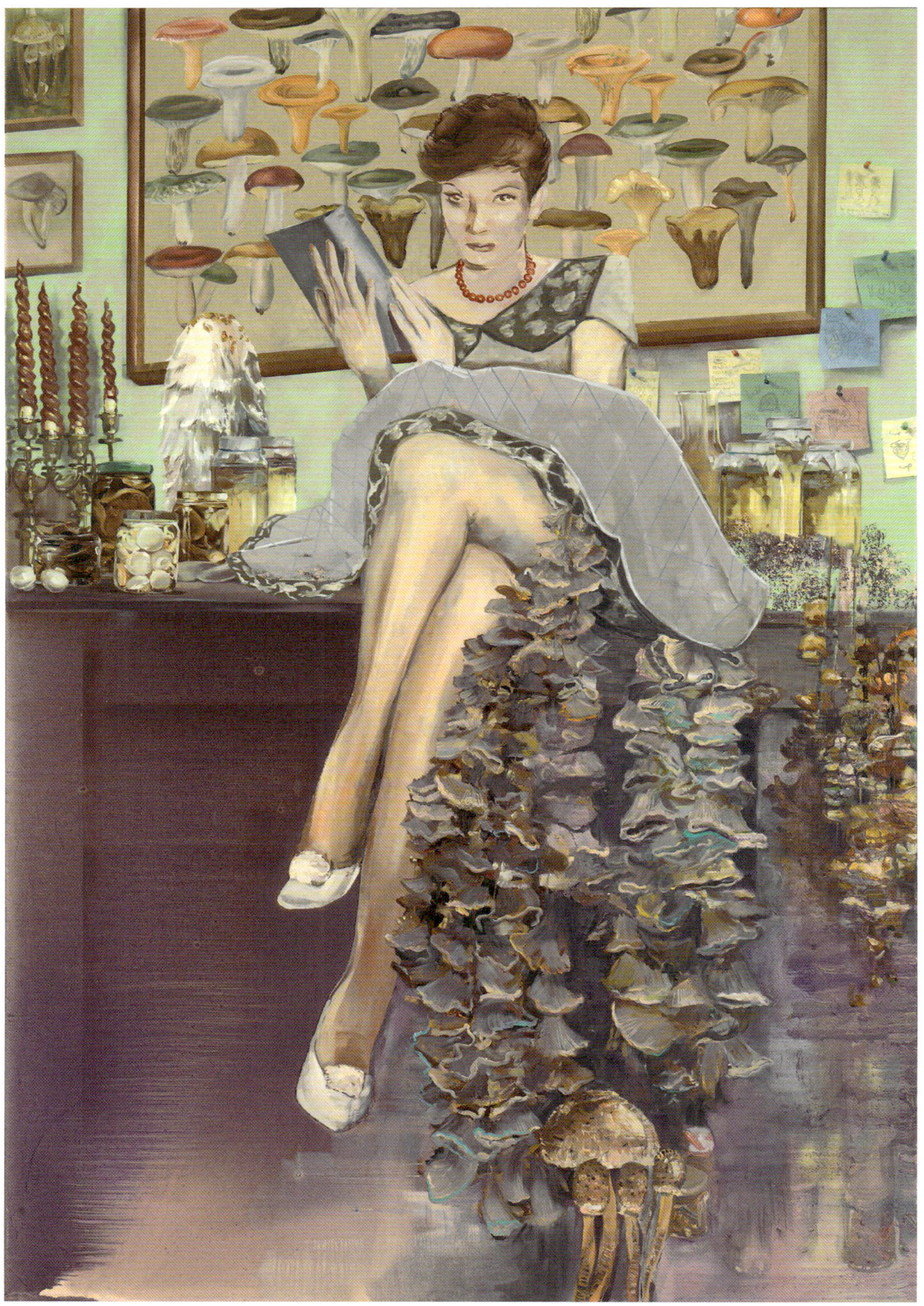

Pauline Olowska
The Alchemist 2015 Oil paint, aerosol paint and graphite on canvas, 2200 × 1500 mm
 Tate, presented by Gaia Art Foundation, UK 2016

'I think a picture is more like the real world when it is made out of the real world.'

– Robert Rauschenberg

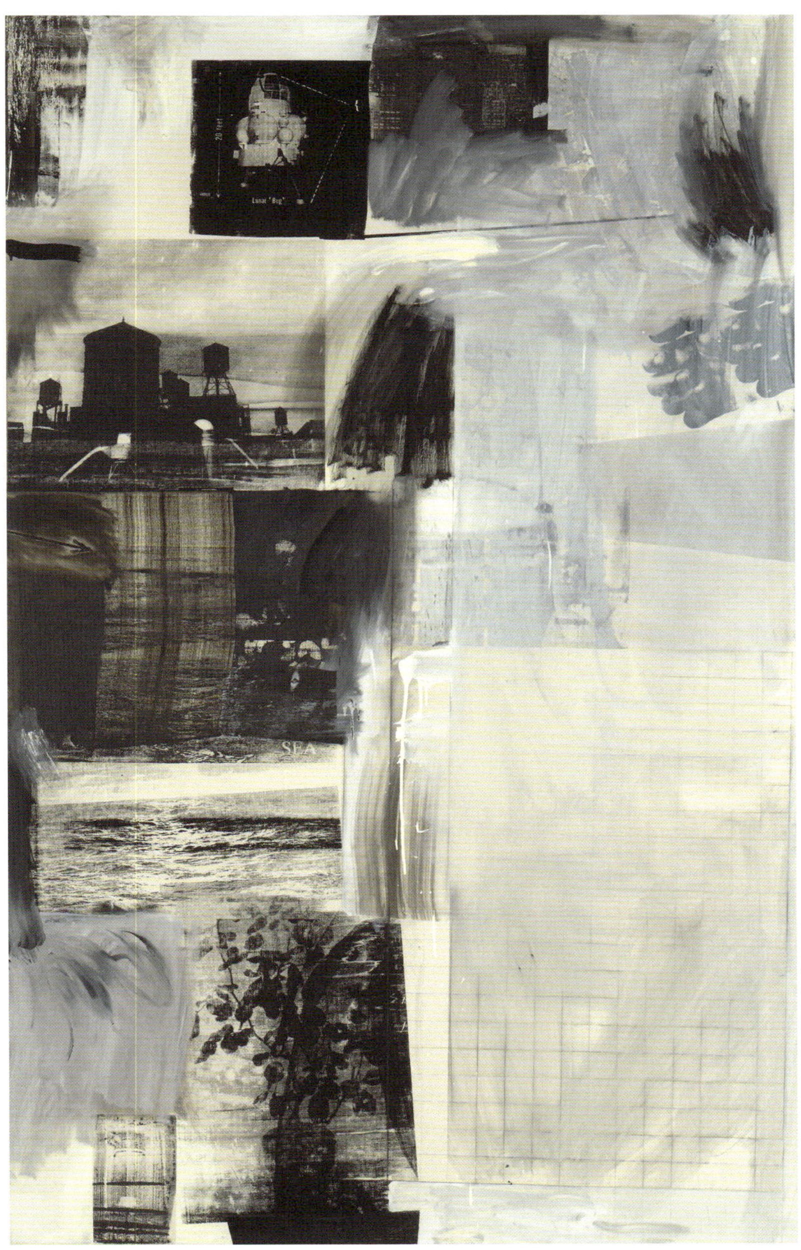

Robert Rauschenberg
Almanac 1962 Oil paint, acrylic paint and screenprint on canvas, 2450 × 1535 × 25 mm
Tate, presented by the Friends of the Tate Gallery 1969

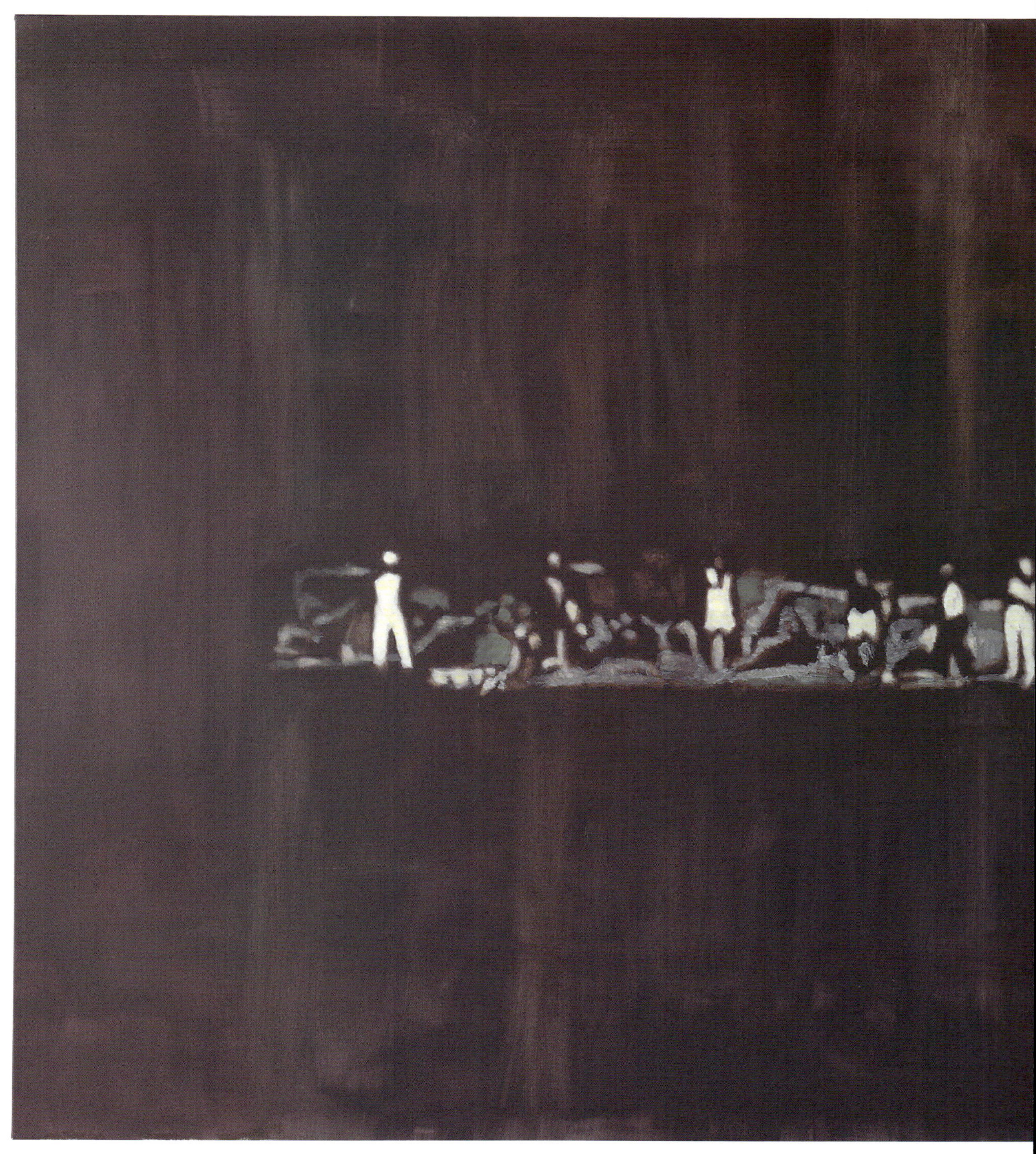

Luc Tuymans
The Shore 2014 Oil paint on canvas, 1945 × 3590 × 45 mm
Tate, presented by the artist 2015

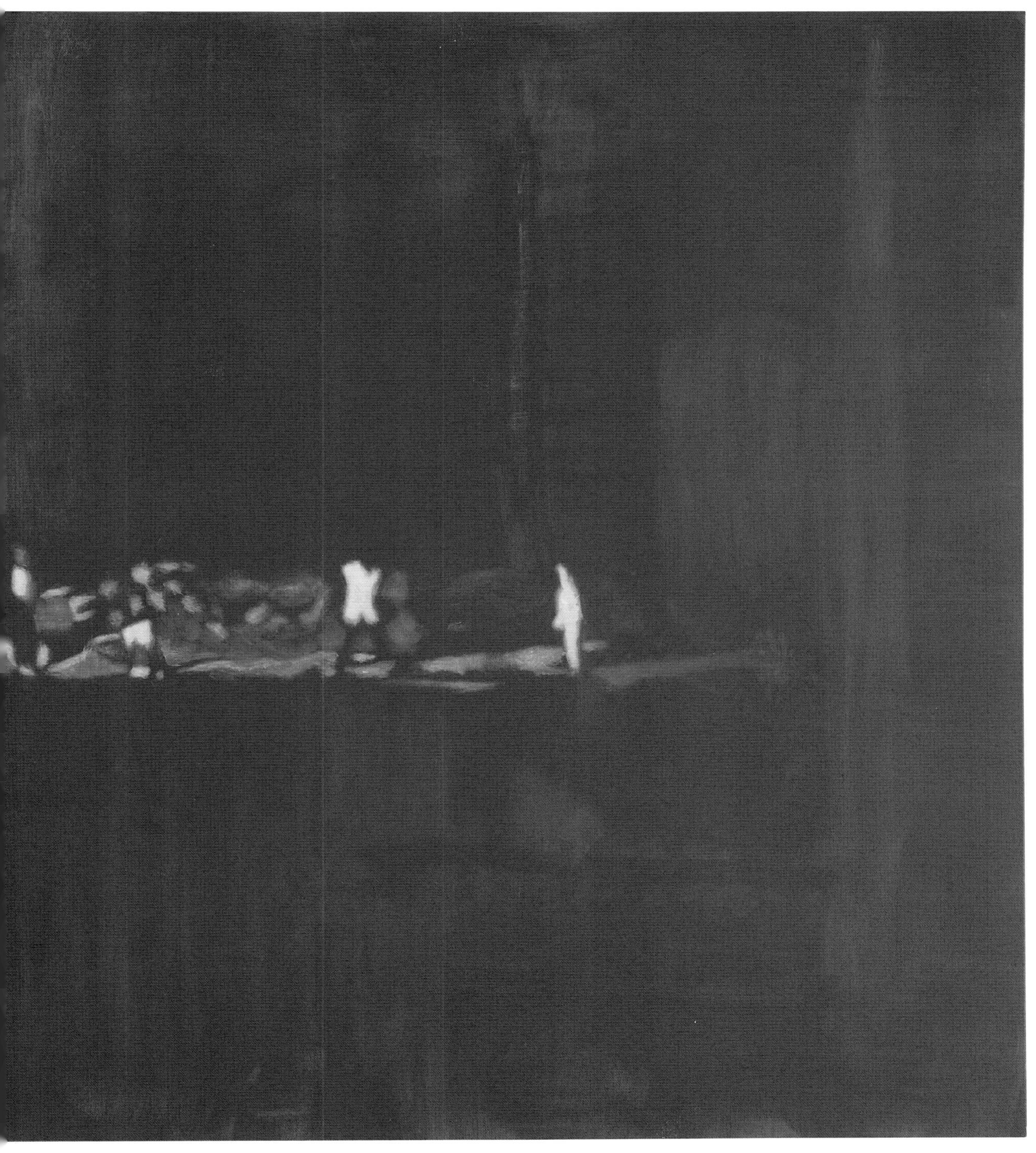

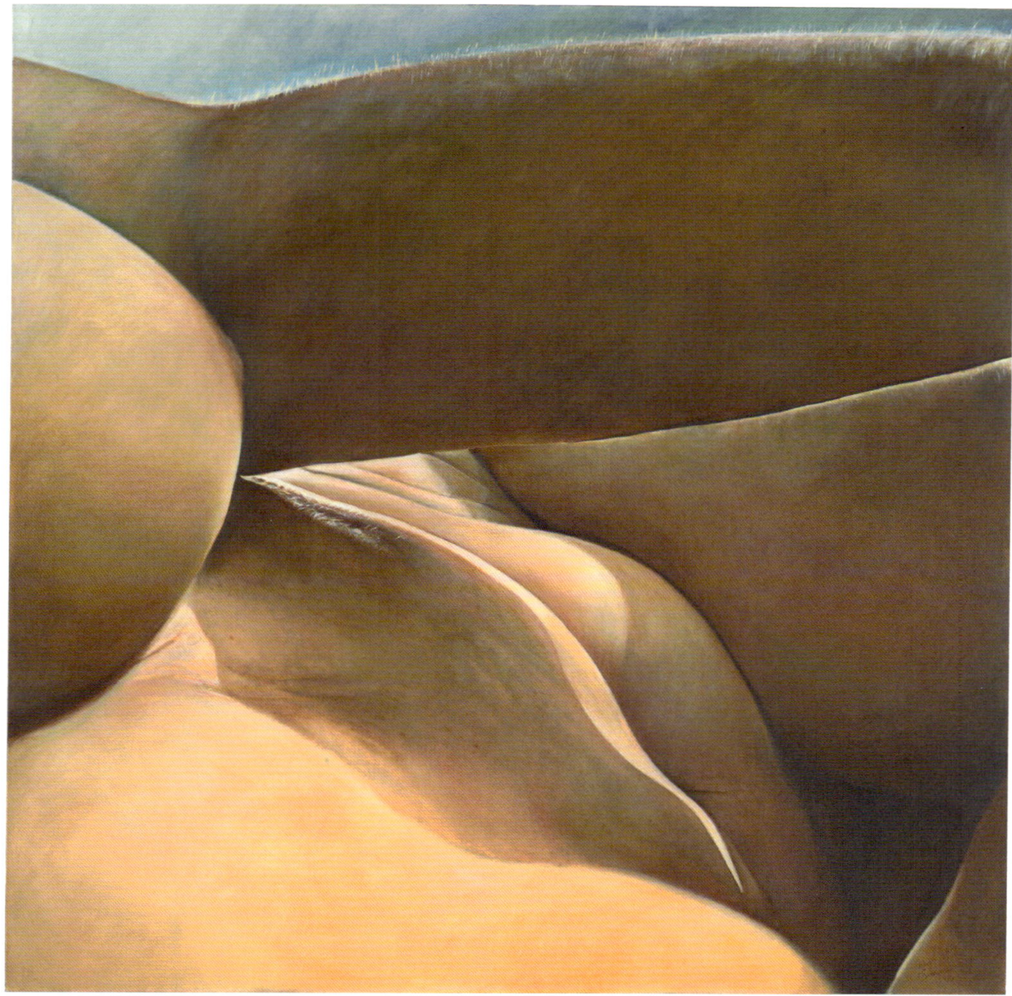

Joan Semmel
Secret Spaces 1976 Oil paint on canvas, 1780 × 1760 mm
Tate, presented by David and Maria Wilkinson (Tate Americas Foundation) 2016, accessioned 2021

Joan Semmel
Secret Spaces 1976
Jo Applin

Secret Spaces belongs to a series of 'self-images' the American artist Joan Semmel painted between 1974 and 1979. Despite its size (the canvas is nearly two metres square), it is an intimate painting in every sense. Semmel's forty-four-year-old naked body lies propped on one side, curled into a soft muddle of flesh and limbs. We don't see the artist's face (or her hands or feet, for that matter) – focus remains on the fleshy form. Sunlight spills in from off-frame, illuminating the fine hairs on her exposed arm, which are almost photographic in their precision. The skin is variously stretched taut and hanging loose. The body spans the canvas in a landscape of mounds, dips and creases – those 'secret spaces' alluded to in the painting's title.

As with many of Semmel's most-known works, *Secret Spaces* is a nude self-portrait based on a photograph taken by the artist. The origin of the image lingers on the canvas through the work's composition, which foreshortens, compresses and reorients the body from a distinctly photographic perspective. Like a photograph taken with a shallow depth of field, the contours of Semmel's body are crisp and clear in the background, blurred in the foreground. In this way, *Secret Spaces* is not only a self-portrait, it is also a formal experiment that traffics in abstraction. With its use of foreshortening and close cropping, it isn't always immediately clear what the viewer is looking at. The surprise when a body, or intimate parts of a body, loom into focus creates a jolt of recognition ('What is that a painting of?' I was asked when I had the painting up on my screen to write this piece. 'A body', I replied, causing a blush of embarrassment when, in a moment of over-correction, they misread the fleshy folds of the stomach as a vulva). When the art historian Richard Meyer asked Semmel whether she found it embarrassing having people look at such intimate depictions of her naked body, she pointed out his mistake in conflating the work of art with the artist: 'These are paintings on canvas, compositions worked up over time. They're not me'.[1]

Semmel was born in the Bronx, New York, in 1932. After graduating from the Pratt Institute in 1963, she moved to Spain, where she lived for seven years, making abstract expressionist, quasi-surrealist paintings. In 1970, Semmel returned to New York to complete an MFA. This was when she began painting in a figurative mode directly from photographs – capturing first with a camera, then translating onto canvas, technicolour scenes of naked, heterosexual couples (mainly friends), creating works which unofficially became known as her 'fuck paintings'. For Semmel, these were insistently feminist paintings, in which 'the act of love is no longer accepted as one of exploitation and submission, but rather as the coming together of two people, equally participating and desirous, each demanding and each giving'.[2] Semmel wrote that, at the time she was producing these erotic works, 'the use of photography by a painter was considered not quite legitimate'. But, by 'appropriat[ing] the modelled form and smooth surface of the closely cropped photograph' into her paintings, she created 'a 'distancing device defining the object as art, and separating it from the realm of pornography'.[3]

This important division relates to one of Semmel's motivations for her turn to erotic imagery, which was to create a counter to the explicit photographs she was seeing on the newsstands on her return to New York from Spain, filled with 'girlie magazines' in which women were reduced to objects of male desire. 'My intention has been to subvert the tradition of the passive female nude', she said.[4] Semmel wanted instead to find 'an erotic language to which women could respond', reassigning a sense of agency and power to a female body not solely in thrall to the male gaze.[5] Indeed, Semmel rejected offers to have her 'fuck paintings' reproduced in *Penthouse* and *Playboy*.[6]

Semmel's work may have a long art-historical trajectory, but with its sharp awareness of gendered power dynamics and insistence on making visible 'issues of women's sexuality and self-image', it spoke powerfully to its contemporary moment.[7] Semmel painted *Secret Spaces* at the height of the women's liberation movement, coinciding with what she called her 'then-emerging consciousness as a feminist'.[8] She was a member of the Ad Hoc Committee of Women Artists, the Art Workers' Coalition and the Fight Censorship Group, whose membership included Louise Bourgeois, Hannah Wilke, Martha Edelheit, Anita Steckel and Judith Bernstein. At a time when women were campaigning for freedom of expression and visibility in public as well as within the art world, Fight Censorship insisted on the right of women artists to depict sexually explicit subject matter. A few years before she painted *Secret Spaces*, Semmel was struggling to find a gallery that would show her 'fuck paintings'.

Produced at a time when painting was often considered a medium unsuited to capturing the urgency of the contemporary moment, *Secret Spaces* straddles the fault lines not only between painting and photography but between private and public. Although an intimate self-portrait, the work implies that the lived, bodily experience of women – of all women, of all bodies – matters. The artist's body fills the canvas, demanding attention. In so doing, Semmel grants the body – and, in later works, the ageing female body – an uncompromising and defiant visibility.

‘I never experienced my work as figurative; I never thought about being representational as being important, but I thought about the figure as an object – as an icon rather than as representation of any reality.’

– Joan Semmel

Towards
the Digital

How can artists grapple with the visual and emotional possibilities of painting in the digital age? How can the medium accurately respond to our contemporary reality? In recent years, we have seen artists attempting to assimilate history and its relationship to images to offer new ways of understanding the present. New media, the internet and archival material collide with the tradition of Western painting to create timely pictorial languages.

Lorna Simpson, Salman Toor and Christina Quarles draw from broadcast media to represent political struggles: the ongoing legacy of racism and structural violence in the US, the migrant crisis of the US/Mexico border, and our position in a world that constantly bombards us with news of international conflicts. How does our fraught sociopolitical climate shape individual consciousness?

Drawing from lived experience, Toor and Quarles portray the contemporary body as fluid, ambiguous and queer, entangled with others, and inhabiting multiple worlds. Pushing painting towards the edges of representation, Quarles and Laura Owens propose a new mode of mark-making. Whereas gestural painting is traditionally associated with heroic, masculine actions, these artists use digital renderings to create carefully controlled gestures. These marks are no longer tied to the hand of the artist, but are instead connected to the layers of media and images of our information age.

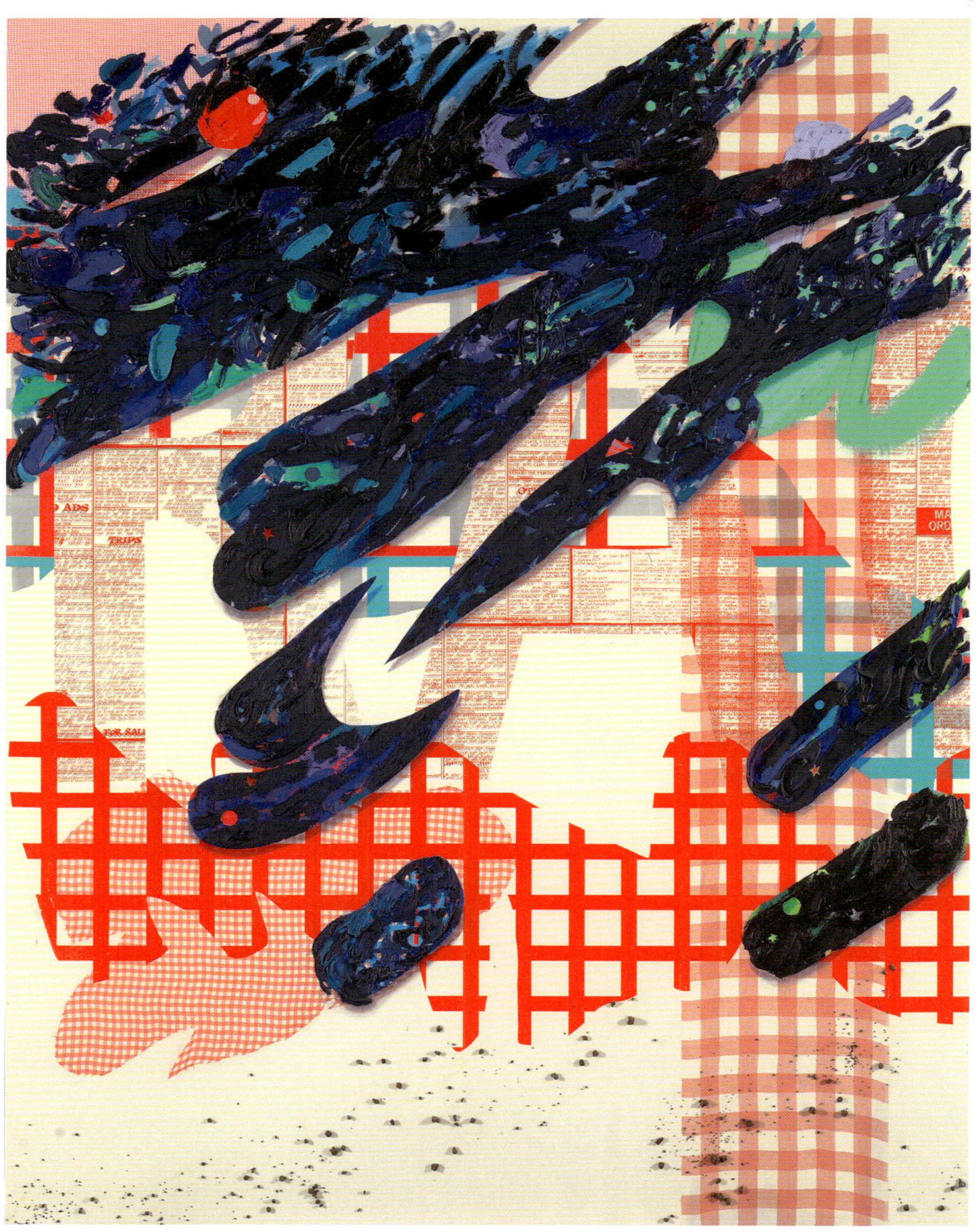

'I feel that the artwork is co-created by the viewer,'
Owens explains, 'I have always thought of it that way.'

– Laura Owens

Laura Owens
Untitled 2012 Oil, acrylic, Flashe, resin, collage and pumice on canvas, 2745 × 2134 × 41 mm
Tate, presented by Sadie Coles HQ 2015

'For me painting is a process of self definition, as an outsider in multiple worlds which become more and more entangled and complex.'

– Salman Toor

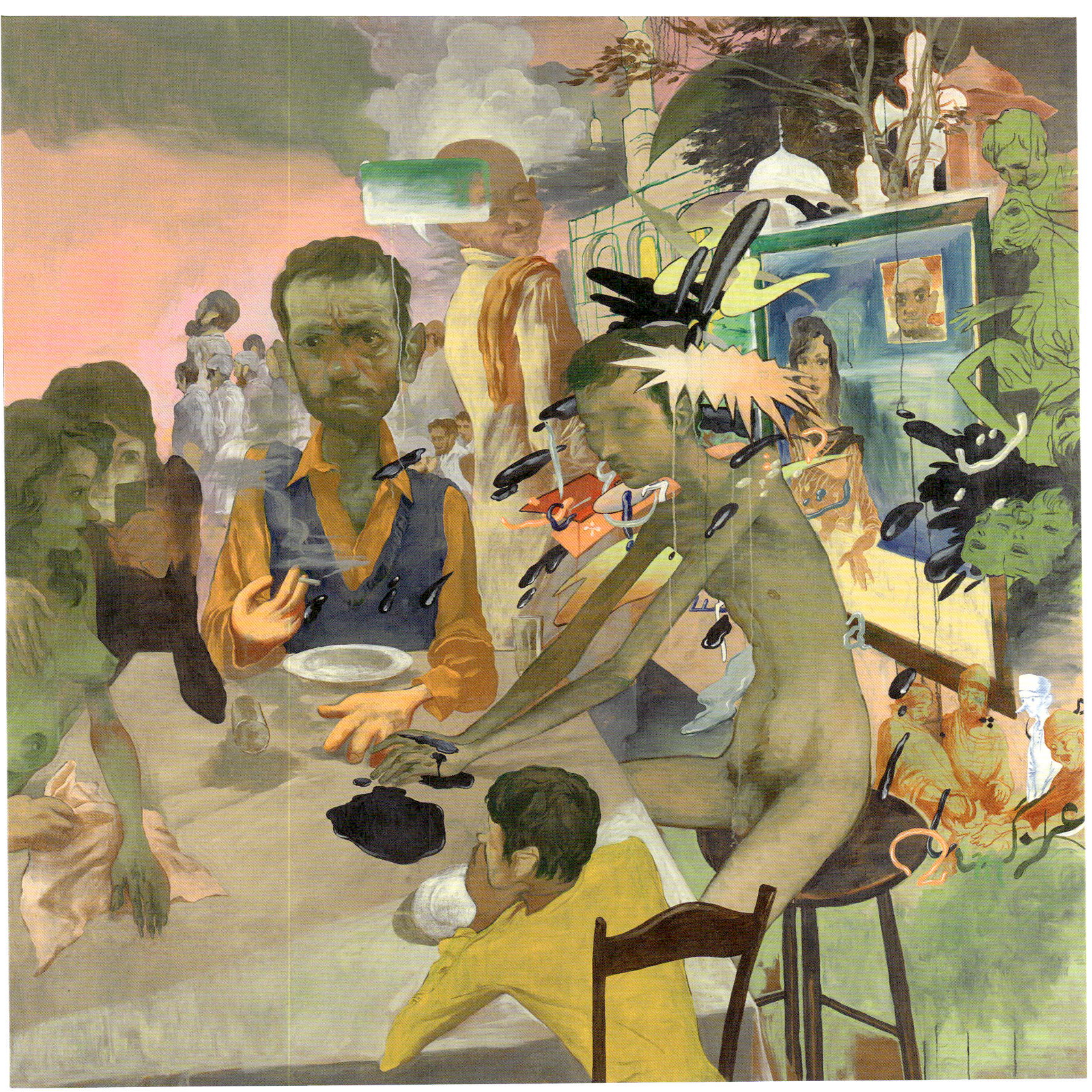

Salman Toor
9PM, the News 2015 Oil paint on canvas, 2503 × 2456 mm
Tate, purchased 2019

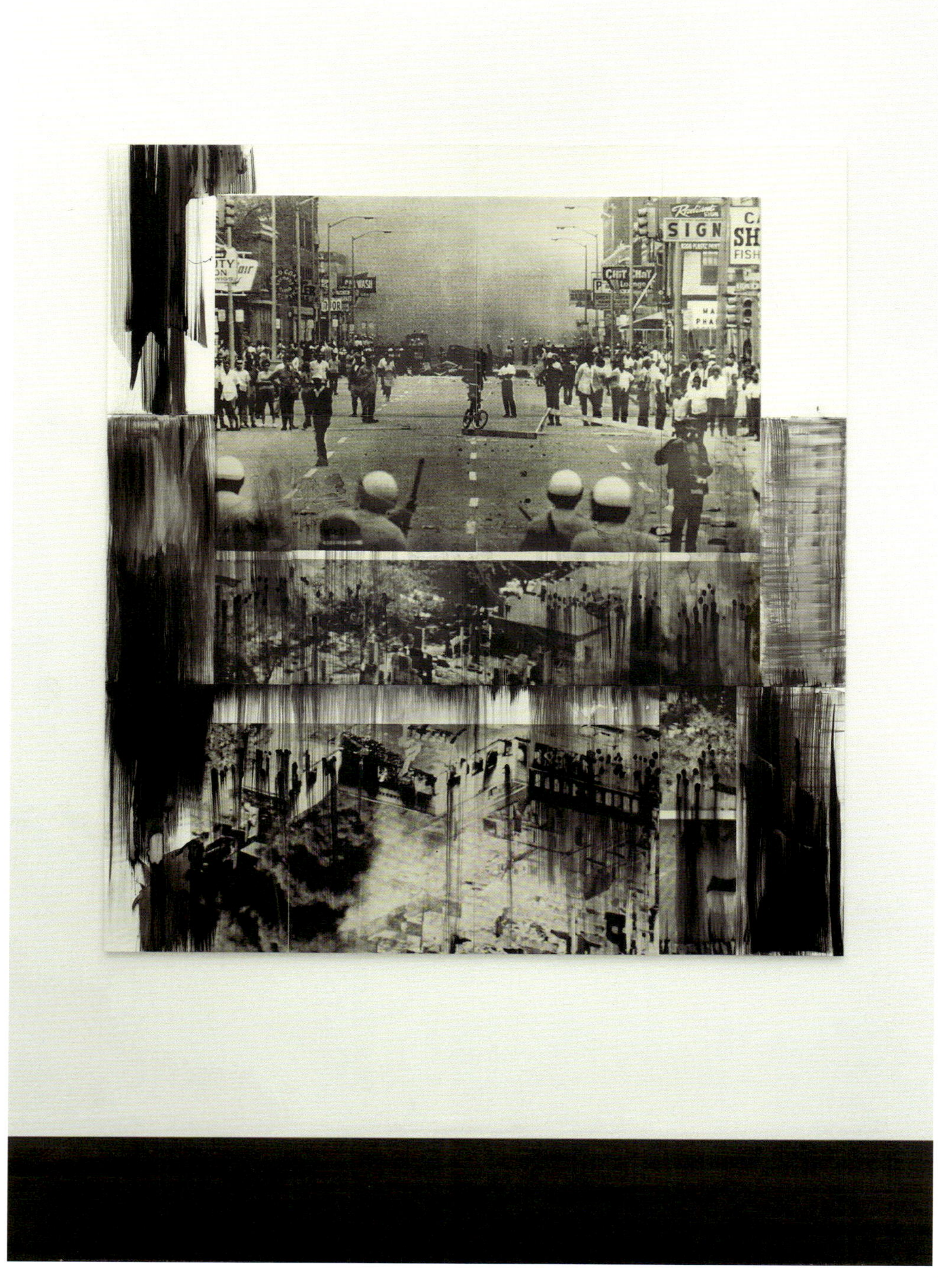

Lorna Simpson
Then & Now 2016 Twelve panels, ink and screenprint on clayboard, 2438 × 2743 mm
Tate, presented by Tate Americas Foundation, purchased using endowment income 2017, accessioned 2021

Lorna Simpson
Then & Now 2016
Vanessa Peterson

Lorna Simpson's *Then & Now* utilises press photographs from the 1960s as a springboard to interrogate the politics of race in the United States today.

Ideas around Black history, gender and politics have been staples of Simpson's work since she first came to prominence in the 1980s with a practice predominantly rooted in photography. *Then & Now* is part of a larger group of works in which Simpson uses found vintage photographs to interrogate the violence Black people have experienced and fought against across generations. To make these works, she digitally enlarges and then screenprints the images onto board or fibreglass before applying washes of richly pigmented ink that partially obscure the image, creating a haunting sense of ambiguity. Simpson at first approached painting 'from a place of intimidation',[1] as she had not painted since her time at art school, several decades before embarking on these works.[2] However, with its deft union of photographic images and ink, *Then & Now* offers an assured and nuanced perspective on what it means to look at what has happened before to make sense of our present reality.

Then & Now comprises twelve individual panels screenprinted with two photographs – one occupying the piece's upper half, with the other inverted directly beneath it. Although not specified, the images are from the 1967 Detroit riots, taken by a photographer for the Detroit Free Press. In the top image, a scattered crowd of Black Americans stands opposite a group of armed policemen in a riot-ravaged street. The image in the work's lower portion is taken from an aerial perspective and depicts smoke billowing from burning buildings. In the border around these images, Lorna has applied dense, broad sweeps of black ink, with softer brushstrokes and sharp, dabbed marks across the lower photograph, from which ink runs vertically down the frame.

The riots were a seismic political event in the history of the United States, taking place against the backdrop of the long, hot summer of 1967. Over 150 urban uprisings erupted across the country that year, protesting institutionalised discrimination, unemployment, poor housing and an abusive police force.[3] Detroit's riots (locally referred to as a rebellion) began in the early morning of 23 July after police raided an illegal club in the city, arresting over eighty Black Americans.[4] Bystanders noted the sound of gunshots during the raid, and there were reported instances of police brutality and violence.[5] Lasting five days and leading to more than 7,000 arrests, the riots were the country's deadliest that year. (According to a 1997 *New York Times* article, 'a Presidential commission later attributed most of the forty-three deaths to police officers and National Guardsmen who, in the commission's view, had gone out of control.'[6]) Two years before the riots, the Michigan Civil Rights Commission had warned that 'a time bomb was ticking', as segregation in housing and education in Detroit, as well as instances of police brutality, were 'the ingredients for potential civil disorder'.[7]

In the Associated Press's curated collection of photographs from Detroit's riots, one caption notes the city's 'decline' after the uprisings, as the upwardly mobile middle classes sought a new life outside of the city: 'Detroit was the nation's fourth biggest city in 1960, but would rank 21st by 2016'.[8] AP's image carousel shows plumes of smoke sprawling over highway intersections, National Guardsmen holding rifles aloft as buildings burn in the background, protestors running down debris-filled streets, and elegant, well-coiffed Black women being escorted into vans and trucks after their arrests.

The 'then' and 'now' Simpson alludes to in this work's title becomes particularly resonant when one considers that it was produced the same year that Donald Trump was elected president of the United States, the lead-up to which was marked by protests across the country responding to his overt bigotry. Earlier that year, protests flared in Milwaukee, Wisconsin, after a young Black man, Sylville Smith, was fatally shot by police, with protesters echoing the frustrations raised in 1967 (Milwaukee then had the highest Black unemployment rate in the country). In Charlotte, North Carolina, another young Black man, Keith Lamont Scott, was shot dead by police that same year. In Baltimore in 2015, residents took to the streets to protest after the death of Freddie Gray, who died in police custody. In 2014, Michael Brown, a Black teenager, was shot and killed by a white police officer in Ferguson, Missouri.

In an interview with writer and curator Antwaun Sargent, Simpson notes that protests such as these and the Ferguson unrest of 2014 'became a jumping-off point' for works like *Then & Now*.[9] It's hard not to see the parallels between the civil rights movement and the ways Black Americans took to the streets to voice discontent and seek change in the 2010s and the Black Lives Matter movement, which, in 2020, saw tens of millions of people participating in thousands of demonstrations across the United States alongside worldwide mass protests.

The injustices raised by Black Americans in 1967 remain equally relevant over five decades on, as racial discrimination continues to impact and shape life in the United States and beyond, and countless images of protest, violence and despair continue to be captured and circulated. *Then & Now*'s potency lies in what we can see as well as what the ink obscures, reminding us of how racial injustice remains part of the landscape of American society today. The past finds its way into the present, then and now.

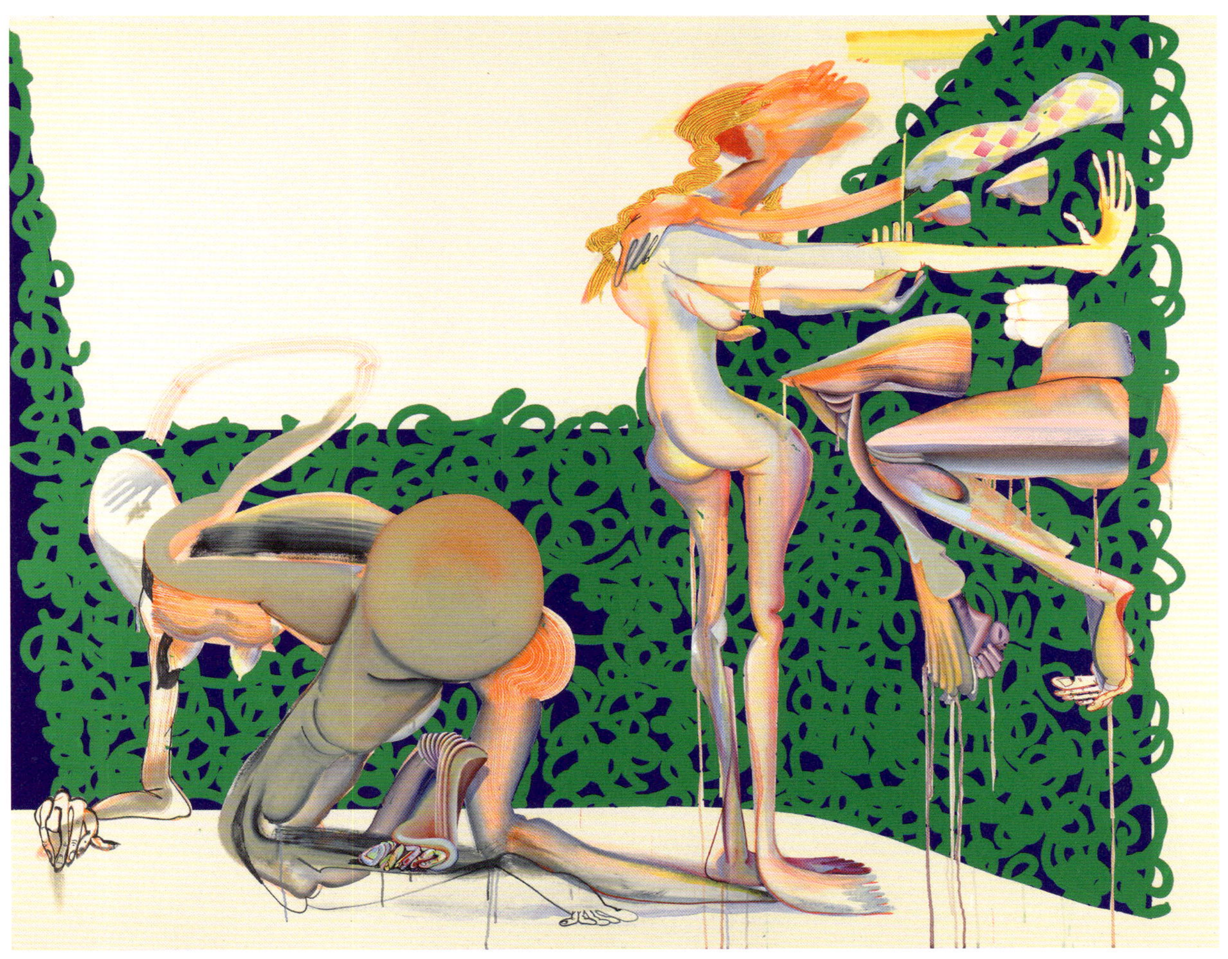

Christina Quarles
Casually Cruel 2018 Acrylic paint on canvas, 1960 × 2443 mm
Tate, presented by Peter Dubens 2019

Notes

Painting in the Time of Photography

1. The artist cited in David Sylvester, *Looking Back at Francis Bacon*, London, 2000, p.98.

The Paradox of the Moment

1. Rosalind Krauss, 'The Photographic Conditions of Surrealism', *October*, vol.19, 1981, p.23.
2. For a commentary on time and photography see Roland Barthes, *Camera Lucida: Reflections on Photography*, New York 1981.
3. Jeff Wall, 'Restoration: Interview with Martin Schwander' (1994), in *Jeff Wall*, London 1996, p.134.
4. Laura Mulvey, '*A Sudden Gust of Wind (After Hokusai)*: From After to Before the Photograph', *Oxford Art Journal*, vol.30, no.1, 1 Mar. 2007, pp.27–37.
5. Lennard J. Davis, 'Migrant Mother: Dorothea Lange and the Truth of Photography', *Los Angeles Review of Books*, 4 Mar. 2020. https://lareviewofbooks.org/article/migrant-mother-dorothea-lange-truth-photography/.
6. Susan Sontag, *On Photography*, London 1978, p.4.
7. John Grierson, *Grierson on Documentary*, ed. Forsyth Hardy, London 1966, p.13.
8. Susan Rosenberg, 'People as Evidence', in *Alice Neel*, exh. cat., Ann Temkin (ed.), Philadelphia Museum of Art, Philadelphia 2000, p.43.
9. *Paula Rego*, exh. cat., Museo Nacional Centro de Arte Reina Sofía, Madrid 2007, p.268.
10. Gerhard Richter, *The Daily Practice of Painting: Writings and Interviews, 1962–1993*, ed. Hans Ulrich Obrist, Cambridge, Mass.; London 1995, p.218.
11. Robert Enright, 'Painting in an Explained Field', *Border Crossings*, August 2018, pp.80–93.
12. Christina Elizabeth Sharpe, *In the Wake: On Blackness and Being*, Durham 2016, p.13.
13. Ibid., p.9.

Alice Neel
Puerto Rican Boys on 108th Street 1955

1. Phoebe Hoban, *Alice Neel: The Art of Not Sitting Pretty*, New York 2010, p.140.
2. While many of the people in Neel's paintings from this period are anonymised, there are also portraits in which the subject's name is recorded in the title, as with her pictures of Georgie Arce, a Puerto Rican boy from the neighbourhood whom Neel painted and sketched a number of times.
3. *Alice Neel*, dir. Andrew Neel, SeeThink Films, New York 2015.
4. Patricia Hills, *Alice Neel*, New York 1983, p.90.
5. Alice Neel Park 01', FBI Records: The Vault. https://vault.fbi.gov/alice-neel.
6. *Alice Neel: People Come First* [podcast], The Met, 9 Mar. 2021. https://www.metmuseum.org/perspectives/articles/2021/3/alice-neel-people-come-first.
7. 'Alice Neel: They Are Their Own Gifts, 1978' [online video], The Met, 18 Dec. 2020. https://youtu.be/MQtSDLOgo5c?si=zy7P-KSYCulRLWRa.
8. 'Alice Neel: Viva la Mujer', *Recording Artists: Radical Women* [podcast], Getty. https://www.getty.edu/recordingartists/season-1/neel/.
9. 'Alice Neel as seen by Hilton Als' [online video], David Zwirner, 10 Jun. 2021. https://youtu.be/2SnAyYprXiA?si=l84lL-ON27qz835T.
10. 'Artists on Their Art', *Art International*, vol.12, no.5, 15 May 1968, p.48.
11. Randall Griffey, 'Painting Fruit(s)', in *Alice Neel: People Come First*, exh. cat., Metropolitan Museum of Art, New York 2021, p.81.

Francis Bacon
Three Studies for Portrait of Lucian Freud 1965

1. 'John Deakin', The Estate of Francis Bacon. https://www.francis-bacon.com/life/family-friends-sitters/john-deakin.
2. Alex Clark, 'Frozen in time: artists at lunch in Wheeler's, March 1963', *Guardian*, 15 Nov. 2015. https://www.theguardian.com/lifeandstyle/2015/nov/15/frozen-in-time-artists-at-lunch-in-wheelers-march-1963.
3. Michael Peppiatt, *Francis Bacon: Anatomy of an Enigma*, London, Sydney, Auckland, Johannesburg 1996, pp.192–3. Cited in 'Lucian Freud', The Estate of Francis Bacon, cited in 'Lucian Freud', The Estate of Francis Bacon. https://www.francis-bacon.com/life/family-friends-sitters/lucian-freud.
4. 'John Deakin', The Estate of Francis Bacon.
5. Ibid.
6. Daniel Farson, *The Gilded Gutter Life of Francis Bacon*, London 1993, pp.238–9. Cited in 'Lucian Freud', The Estate of Francis Bacon.
7. 'Lucian Freud', The Estate of Francis Bacon.
8. Tom Shone, 'Inside the Complicated, Enthralling Friendship of Lucian Freud and Francis Bacon', *Avenue*, 18 Jan. 2021. https://avenuemagazine.com/lucian-freud-francis-bacon-friendship-new-biographies/.
9. Dalya Alberge, 'Secret tapes shed light on Francis Bacon's bitter battle with Lucian Freud', *Guardian*, 28 Jan. 2018. https://amp.theguardian.com/artanddesign/2018/jan/28/francis-bacon-secret-tapes-lucian-freud-battle.
10. Ibid.
11. Ibid.
12. Michel Archimbaud, *Francis Bacon In Conversation with Michel Archimbaud*, London 1993, p.72. Cited in 'Lucian Freud', The Estate of Francis Bacon.
13. 'Francis Bacon – The South Bank Show (1985)' [online video], *Under Pressure Magazine*, 28 Sept. 2015. https://vimeo.com/140651929.

Hiroshi Sugimoto
Aegean Sea, Pilion 1990; Tyrrhenian Sea, Scilla 1993; Ligurian Sea 1993; Tyrrhenian Sea, Conca 1994

1. Karen Chernick, 'Hiroshi Sugimoto: Photography That Fools the Eye', *Art & Object*, 28 Jan. 2019. https://www.artandobject.com/articles/hiroshi-sugimoto-photography-fools-eye.
2. 'Hiroshi Sugimoto Interview: Between Sea and Sky', Louisiana Channel, 11 Sept. 2018. https://www.youtube.com/watch?v=JWh4t67e5GM.
3. Emily McDermott, 'Hiroshi Sugimoto's Future', *Interview*, 11 Feb. 2016. https://www.interviewmagazine.com/art/hiroshi-sugimoto-sea-of-buddha-pace.

Andy Warhol
Self Portrait 1966–7

1. Andy Warhol, *The Philosophy of Andy Warhol (From A to B and Back Again)*, 1975.
2. Blake Gopnik, *Warhol: A Life as Art*, London 2020, p.372.
3. Paul Carroll, 'What's a Warhol?', *Playboy*, September 1969.

Miriam Cahn
The Beautiful Blue (Das Schöne Blau), 2008–17

1. Daniel Trilling, 'How the media contributed to the migrant crisis', *Guardian*, 1 Aug. 2019. https://www.theguardian.com/news/2019/aug/01/media-framed-migrant-crisis-disaster-reporting. Adapted from an essay in *Lost in Media: Migrant Perspectives and the Public Sphere*, eds. Ismail Einashe and Thomas Roueché, Amsterdam 2019.
2. By 2022, the global situation had worsened, with the UN reporting that over 100 million people were forcibly displaced. 'More than 100 million now forcibly displaced: UNHCR report', UN News, 16 Jun. 2022. https://news.un.org/en/story/2022/06/1120542.
3. Devorah Lauter, '"It's Society's Problem, and That's Why It's Interesting": Artist Miriam Cahn on Painting Controversial Subjects in an Age of Correctness', *Artnet*, 18 July 2022. https://news.artnet.com/art-world/miriam-cahn-profile-2143197.
4. Myria Georgiou and Rafal Zaborowski, 'Media coverage of the "refugee crisis": A cross-European perspective', The Council of Europe, 2017. https://rm.coe.int/1680706b00
5. *Lost in Media: Migrant Perspectives and the Public Sphere*, eds. Ismail Einashe and Thomas Roueché, Amsterdam 2019.
6. Chris Tomlinson, '"Invasion": 5,000 Illegal Migrants Arrive in Lampedusa in One Day', *European Conservative*, 14 Sept. 2023. https://europeanconservative.com/articles/news/

invasion-5000-illegal-migrants-arrive-in-
lampedusa-in-one-day/.
7. Philip Pullella, 'No "sea of death": Pope calls
for pan-European action on migration', *Reuters*,
23 Sept. 2023. https://www.reuters.com/world/
europe/no-sea-death-pope-calls-pan-european-
action-migration-2023-09-23/.
8. Lauter 2022.
9. James Cahill, *Maggi Hambling: Edge*, exh. cat,
Marlborough Fine Art, London 2017.
10. Ismail Einashe, *Look Again: Strangers*, London
2023.

David Hockney
Portrait of an Artist (Pool with Two Figures) 1972

1. David Hockney, *David Hockney by David
Hockney: My Early Years*, ed. Nikos Stangos,
London 1976, p.247.
2. Ibid.
3. Martin Gayford, *A Bigger Message: Conversations
with David Hockney*, London 2011, p.195.
4. Roberta Smith, 'David Hockney's Life in
Painting: Spare, Exuberant, Full', *New York Times*,
23 Nov. 2017. https://www.nytimes.com/2017/
11/23/arts/design/david-hockney-art-review-
metropolitan-museum-of-art.html.
5. Hockney 1976, p.240.
6. Quoted in Ed Helmore, '$90m David Hockney
is not a "break-up picture", says ex-lover',
Guardian, 18 Nov. 2018. https://www.
theguardian.com/artanddesign/2018/nov/18/
david-hockney-pool-portrait-peter-schlesinger-
ex-lover-speaks.
7. Gayford 2011, p.50.
8. Ibid. p.234.
9. Hockney 1976, p.247.

Joan Semmel
Secret Spaces 1976

1. Richard Meyer, 'Body of Painting', in *Solitaire:
Lee Lozano, Sylvia Plimack Mangold, Joan Semmel*,
exh cat., Helen Molesworth (ed.), Wexner
Center for the Arts Ohio State University,
Columbus 2008, p.112.
2. Joan Semmel and April Kingsley, 'Sexual
Imagery in Women's Art', *Woman's Art Journal*,
Spring–Summer 1980, vol.1, no.1, pp.1–6.
3. Daphne Merkin, 'Joan Semmel Takes an
Unflinching View of Her Own Body', *New York
Times Style Magazine*, 17 Dec. 2021. https://www.
nytimes.com/2021/12/09/t-magazine/joan-
semmel-nude-portraits.html.
4. Meyer 2008, p.113.
5. Richard Meyer, 'Camera Eye: The Art of Joan
Semmel', *Artforum*, Sept. 2013. https://www.
artforum.com/print/201307/camera-eye-the-
art-of-joan-semmel-42645.
6. Ibid.
7. Meyer 2008, p.112.

8. *Paintings by Joan Semmel*, exh. cat., Jorgensen
Gallery, University of Connecticut, Storrs 1978,
p.24.

Lorna Simpson
Then & Now 2016

1. Andrianna Campbell, 'Lorna Simpson',
Artforum, 26 Nov. 2016. https://www.artforum.
com/interviews/lorna-simpson-talks-about-
her-recent-paintings-and-solo-exhibition-in-
fort-worth-64979.
2. Siddhartha Mitter, 'Lorna Simpson Embraces
the Blues', *New York Times*, 13 Jun. 2019. https://
www.nytimes.com/2019/06/13/arts/design/
lorna-simpson-paintings-hauser-wirth.html.
3. Robyn Meredith, '5 Days in 1967 Still
Shake Detroit', *New York Times*, 23 Jul. 1997.
https://www.nytimes.com/1997/07/23/
us/5-days-in-1967-still-shake-detroit.html.
4. Michael T. Luongo, 'Detroit Museums Examine
the Riots That Changed the City', *New York Times*,
13 Aug. 2017. https://www.nytimes.com/2017/08/
13/arts/design/detroit-museums-examine-1967-
riots.html.
5. Lorraine Boissoneault, 'Understanding
Detroit's 1967 Upheaval 50 Years Later',
Smithsonian, 26 Jul. 2017. https://www.
smithsonianmag.com/history/understanding-
detroits-1967-upheaval-50-years-later-
180964212/.
6. Meredith 1997.
7. Matthew D. Lassiter and the Policing and Social
Justice History Lab, 'Uprising and Occupation,
1967', *Detroit Under Fire: Police Violence, Crime
Politics, and the Struggle for Racial Justice in
the Civil Rights Era*, University of Michigan
Carceral State Project, 2021. https://policing.
umhistorylabs.lsa.umich.edu/s/detroitunderfire/
page/1967.
8. '50 years on, AP photos show violence of
Detroit's riots', Associated Press, 16 Jul. 2017.
https://apnews.com/article/north-america-us-
news-riots-1967-riots-detroit-d352bd0377324b
95be0def4db89e3f36.
9. Antwaun Sargent, 'Lorna Simpson Shifts
Gears', *Cultured*, 8 Sept. 2016. https://www.
culturedmag.com/article/2016/09/08/lorna-
simpson-salon-94.

First published 2023 by order of the Tate Trustees
by Tate Publishing, a division of Tate Enterprises Ltd,
Millbank, London SW1P 4RG
www.tate.org.uk/publishing

on the occasion of the exhibition
Capturing the Moment

Tate Modern, London
15 June 2023 – 28 April 2024

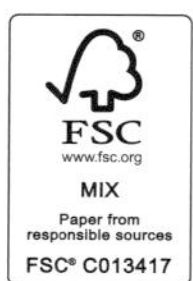

Capturing the Moment is realised in collaboration with
the YAGEO Foundation, Taiwan. The YAGEO
Foundation was founded by Taiwanese collector,
entrepreneur and philanthropist Pierre Chen in 1999.

A catalogue record for this book is available from
the British Library

ISBN 978-1-84976-898-6

Distributed in the United States and Canada by
ABRAMS, New York

Library of Congress Control Number applied for

Project Editor: Emma Capps
Production: Bill Jones
Picture Researcher: Bill Jones
Designed by Joe Hales
assisted by Sam Eccles, Joe Hales studio
Colour reproduction by DL Imaging, London
Printed and bound in Wales by Cambrian Printers

FRONT COVER: Andy Warhol, *Self-Portrait 1966–67*
(modified detail from the original) as seen on p.84

Measurements of artworks are given in millimeters,
height before width